DO SOME THING!

Make Your Life Count

Miles McPherson

BakerBooks

a division of Baker Publishing Group
Grand Rapids, Michigan

© 2009 by Miles McPherson

Published by Baker Books
a division of Baker Publishing Group
P.O. Box 6287, Grand Rapids, MI 49516-6287
www.bakerbooks.com

Printed in the United States of America

The Library of Congress Cataloging-in-Publication Data
McPherson, Miles.
    Do something! : make your life count / Miles McPherson.
        p.   cm.
    ISBN 978-0-8010-1332-4 (cloth)
    1. Christian life. I. Title.
BV4501.3.M3787 2009
248—dc22   2009026787

ISBN 978-0-8010-7274-1 (ITPE)

Unless otherwise indicated, Scripture is taken from the New King James Version. Copyright © 1982 by Thomas Nelson, Inc. Used by permission. All rights reserved.

Scripture marked NASB is taken from the New American Standard Bible®, Copyright © 1960, 1962, 1963, 1968, 1971, 1972, 1973, 1975, 1977, 1995 by The Lockman Foundation. Used by permission.

Scripture marked NIV is taken from the HOLY BIBLE, NEW INTERNATIONAL VERSION®. NIV®. Copyright © 1973, 1978, 1984 by International Bible Society. Used by permission of Zondervan. All rights reserved.

Published in association with Yates & Yates (www.yates2.com).

09   10   11   12   13   14   15   7   6   5   4   3   2   1

To my parents, Gene and Margaret, who raised me better than they know. Their love and friendship to this day keep me committed to finish strong.

To my wife and family, Debbie, Kelly, Kimmie, and Miles, for being very patient with my crazy schedule. The "Five McPees" keep my feet on the ground.

To my staff whose tireless work God uses to bring about supernatural ministry each day.

Finally, I want to dedicate this book to the potential that God has assigned to you, the reader. God's dream for your life is screaming to come out and *do something* good for someone in need. My prayer is that as you read this book you give your potential the **freedom** to speak to you, inspire you, and move you to DO Something.

Contents

Part 4   Pain: *It Doesn't Have to Only Hurt*

Part 5   Power: *The Ability to DO*

Part 6   Passion: *Never Give Up*

Introduction

I walked directly behind the nurse without looking left or right. She was leading me through the intensive care unit. All I could hear was the hissing of ventilators, the *beep-beep-beep* of heart monitors, and the whispers of other nurses. I kept my eyes straight ahead and ignored the knot in my stomach.

A church member had asked me to visit a twenty-five-year-old woman named Tracy who had been in a terrible car accident. Of course I would. That's what pastors do. I thought I was prepared.

The nurse stopped, and I glanced up. There. *Oh no*. That had to be Tracy.

The young woman lay flat, with a bunch of tubes coming out of her body and running into a machine. Small chains and straps from an overhead frame suspended her swollen arms, burned black and pink. Both legs were in straps too, and pointed toward the ceiling. Her knees were wrapped in white gauze. That's where they had been amputated.

As I got closer, I noticed Tracy's chest was bare. My eyes traveled up to her head. Chunks of blond hair had been burned away. One eye was completely swollen shut. The other one stared at me.

I imagined she had lots to say. *Who are you? What do you want? Somebody please cover me up*.

It was my first hospital visit as a young minister. I was a professional-football-player-turned-youth-pastor. And I was clueless.

I took another step forward and leaned down, introducing myself. I offered to pray for her.

Around the tube in her mouth, the young woman mumbled something.

"Can I get you something?" I asked.

She shook her head and mumbled again, this time a little louder.

I glanced around for the nurse, who was doing something a couple of beds away, and then asked, "Are you trying to tell me something?"

She shook her head and mumbled louder.

Again I asked, "Do you want me to leave?"

Again Tracy shook her head. This time she began to groan. She started to rattle her arms and what was left of her legs.

The nurse walked over and glared at me, as if I'd yanked on Tracy's chains or something. She draped a towel over her chest. I swallowed and moved to the other side of the bed as she tried to calm Tracy down. But Tracy wouldn't stop shaking and moaning. The nurse kept glancing at me with a disgusted look on her face.

I looked over my shoulder toward the door. That's where I wanted to be: through that door and gone. *I am in shape*, I thought irrationally. *I can jump this bed behind me and run out of here . . .*

Then an orderly rolled in a gurney, right in front of the doorway. I was trapped! It felt like I was in a box full of ants—anxiety was crawling all over me. All of a sudden my vocabulary was one word: *Um . . .*

Thank goodness it wasn't long before the nurse excused me from the room. She saved me. It is one thing to miss a tackle or let a guy catch a touchdown pass. But this was failure on a much higher level.

I remember walking to my car as fast as I could without breaking into a sprint. I wanted so bad to hide my Bible under my shirt. I was sweating with shame. *I have no business claiming to be some pastor.* God sent me there to encourage that girl. I failed her—and Him.

Why couldn't I do something for her?

I eventually realized that before I could *do something* for Tracy, I needed first to *do something* for myself.

Before You Can Do Anything

I had walked into the hospital as "Joe Pastor," the guy with all of the answers, on a self-righteous mission to *do something* good for someone in need.

But I was missing a huge step. I should have left the pastor title in the car. I should have walked into Tracy's hospital room as a broken man who had spent time in my own spiritual "hospital bed." Instead of expecting to do something *for* her, I should have come to do something *with* her: to *hurt*.

I should have known better too. After all, I had hurt before, both alone and alongside others.

At one point as a young man playing professional football with the NFL, I was living the dream—and dying a nightmare of a cocaine habit. I was cut from NFL teams three times, and God miraculously delivered me from my addiction in one day. I'll give you the dirty details later in the book.

I eventually made a commitment to serve the Lord and not myself. I had no idea what was in store. I became a youth pastor and evangelist, and eventually started the Rock Church. By our nine-year anniversary, we had become one of the nation's fastest-growing churches—which simply means we have a lot of responsibility for a lot of hurting people.

I have, in my own small way, been Tracy. And I have seen many Tracys—people whose lives have been destroyed by car accidents, severed relationships, paralyzing pride, brutal addictions, and smashed careers.

The only reason many of them survived their tragedy is because along the way there were people willing to do something and share the lessons of their own brokenness.

Making Your Life Count

The world needs you. It's broken.

Look around you. We're facing economic chaos, endless wars, AIDS, famine, ecological ruin, political corruption—the list is endless. Your neighbors are in desperate need of love and a helping hand.

It's my belief that what the world needs is God's love. But whether or not you share my Christian beliefs, you can recognize that someone needs to do something. Right now!

That someone can be you. You were created to do something great. You want your life to count, or you wouldn't have picked up this book. There's no better way to make a difference in the world than to take action and help someone out—no matter your age or race, no matter your religion or lack of religion, no matter what.

But there's a step we all need to take first: you and I need to recognize that not only is the world broken, but we are broken also.

The Plan

Through the years I have gained insights from the life of Jesus Christ on how I can do something to make my life count and to help people in need. These insights might save you some time and energy.

I asked myself, if Jesus was God—holy and perfect—why couldn't He just have revealed Himself as God and then died, say, a week later?

Wouldn't that have been enough to pay for our sins? He was sinless, after all. His sacrifice would have been acceptable. Why three years of ministry? Why teach the lessons? Why perform the miracles? Why be denied, why be betrayed, why suffer a horrible death?

The reasons are many, but here's the one I want us to focus on. He was on earth to do more than to accomplish the sacrifice on the cross.

Jesus came to launch a *plan*.

Jesus' plan would not only secure salvation for those who would believe but would establish a foundation for *us* to execute *our* individual roles in the plan of salvation for others.

One way to look at this master plan, and apply it to our lives, is to divide it into five parts. Being the preacher I am, I have named the parts with labels starting with *P*:

Preparation
Purpose
Pain
Power
Passion

The five P's make up a plan that you and I can follow. This plan empowers us to communicate hope to a broken world. A world that is wounded, critically ill, sustained by life support. A world that has been burned by sin.

Simply put, you and I were created by God to do something great with our lives, something like Jesus did—but not because we are smarter, more special, or better qualified than anyone else. We're not. Whether you accept it or not, you too are broken.

Our spiritual health has been (or perhaps is still) just as compromised as Tracy's physical health was. Our wounds are deep, they are severe, and they are fatal. The only thing separating us from those whose spiritual wounds will kill them is the encounter we have had—or need to have—with the Great Physician and Savior, the Son of God, Jesus Christ.

Until you get in touch with your brokenness, you won't be able to relate to someone else's brokenness. Until you are able to express yourself through your pain, the cries of those we need to help will only sound like mumbling.

Celebrating Our Brokenness

The first thing Jesus did was to do something *with* us: He became a man and subjected Himself to the temptations and struggles of this world. After He identified with our brokenness, He went on to do something *for* us. He died on the cross.

If you want to do something great, keep in mind what Jesus told us to remember. Just before He left, He gave us specific instructions. He said, *Celebrate My brokenness. Celebrate My body, broken for you. Celebrate My blood, spilled for you.* That's what communion is all about.

You see, He could have asked us to remember His resurrection. He could have asked us to honor the miracles He performed, or to practice the way He outsmarted the smartest theologians of the time. No. He said, *Celebrate My brokenness.*

Why? Just as He identified with our brokenness before He did something for us, so we must identify with our brokenness before we can do something for others. We do this by acknowledging our own

11

brokenness and sharing the healing that God is bringing to our lives. Let's keep in mind that our "DO Something" is all about allowing Him to do something *through* us. God has to first do something in you before He can do something through you.

Do you want to do something significant with your life?

Do you want to do what Jesus did?

Here is your chance.

Just as Jesus did something with eternal impact on our behalf, He has left a model for us to do something with eternal impact for those He would send our way.

God's intended ministry in that hospital room that day was not a program but an intersection of what He was doing with my personal brokenness and the brokenness in Tracy's life.

Warning: If you are not willing to be vulnerable with your own brokenness, it will be very difficult, if not impossible, for you to do something of eternal significance for the broken world around you. Don't be like the proud, clueless young minister in that hospital room. Admit that you are broken, and humble yourself. Ask God to begin His healing work in you. It is only then that He will be able to work through you to heal others.

Before you begin, I invite you to hear a word of encouragement from me at www.milesmcpherson.com.

About This Book

This book has six sections, each with five chapters.

Part 1 is the **Plan**: *An Overview of the 5 P's*
Part 2 is about **Preparation**: *Advance Work*
Part 3 is about **Purpose**: *Obedience*
Part 4 is about **Pain**: *It Doesn't Have to Only Hurt*
Part 5 is about **Power**: *The Ability to Do*
Part 6 is about **Passion**: *Never Give Up*

Each chapter has several of the following features:

- *A story from real life.* All of the people you'll meet on these pages are real people (including me!), although a few names have been changed to protect the privacy of the individuals.
- *The life of Christ.* We will focus on an aspect of the life of Christ in each chapter.
- *DO Something activities.* At the end of each chapter you will be challenged to do something practical—to put into practice the principles of the chapter.
- *DO Something heroes.* We'll be highlighting exemplary people throughout the book, including a way to get further information, such as websites.
- *Ph.DO assignments.* For those who want to get an "advanced degree" in doing something, we will provide an assignment

with practical steps online. Ph.DO's are for those who want to start ministries that can provide ongoing *do something* opportunities for themselves and others.

- *Help Wanted* fact boxes.
- *Prayer.* Each chapter ends with a suggested prayer.

You want to make your life count. So, *DO Something* and begin reading!

Part 1

The Plan

An Overview of the 5 P's

No one has done more good in and for this world than Jesus. During His three-year ministry, He established a moral standard for humankind that has yet to be improved upon. He healed the sick, cast demons out of the possessed, and raised the dead. He has a **Plan** for you, and guess what it says?

You were created
to do something great!

· ·

Most assuredly, I say to you, he who believes in Me, the works that I do he will do also; and greater works than these he will do, because I go to My Father.

—John 14:12

1

Donna and Bill

Preparation—Advance Work

For we are His workmanship, created in Christ Jesus for good works, which God prepared beforehand that we should walk in them.

— Ephesians 2:10

Donna was in the kitchen of her *Jungle Book*-bamboo hut when she heard the knock on the door. She put four-month-old Bethy in her high chair and told four-year-old Elisa to stay at the table.

The visitors, whoever they were, were speaking English. *How odd*, she thought. Everyone in the tropical river valley spoke only Palawano, except her husband, Bill, and her.

Bunched up on her stoop were ten brown-skinned, gangsta-looking men carrying automatic weapons. They were dressed in green fatigues darkened by sweat from the 90-degree heat and 80 percent humidity. Grenades hung from their belts.

The man in front looked up at Donna, a tall, thin blonde from California.

"Where-is-your-husband-Bill-Davis?" he spat out in one breath.

How do they know his name? Donna's heart began to race. *What do they want?*

She pictured her daughters and then Bill, who was alone in a hut at the other end of the grass airstrip, studying the Palawano language.

A young couple from San Diego, Donna and Bill had just moved into the area. Their new home was in a remote spot on Palawan, a province in the Philippines. They felt that they had found the perfect place to fulfill what God had called them to do: plant churches and translate the New Testament into the native language of a people without the Word of God.

Just as God made preparations for Jesus long before He came into the world, so God has made preparations for the great works He has planned for you to do as well.

Like something on *National Geographic*, the lush jungle valley was dotted with three- and four-hut communities, each about a fifteen-minute walk from each other. Not the end of the world, but you could just about see it from there.

What Donna and Bill didn't know was the Moro National Liberation Front (MNLF), a Muslim rebel group, was in the area too.

The men at her door were Filipino and Malaysian members of the MNLF, determined to "liberate" the southern part of Palawan.

"We are moving into this jungle," the young leader said to Donna after she told him Bill wasn't home. "And if you stay out of our business, we will leave you alone. But if you meddle in our affairs, we will kill you."

Donna looked at her kids. *I didn't sign up for this*, she thought.

∙∙

Dozens of people waited in line to get dunked in the water by a creature who looked like an ancient-era Bigfoot. Hair past his shoulders, bushy beard, camel's hair clothing, John the Baptist stood in the middle of the river, pushing them down and pulling them up.

Step by step, people inched through the water closer to John. In and out of the water they went as they repented of their sins.

All of a sudden, John's jaw dropped. He stepped back and froze. Standing face-to-face with Jesus, John did not know what to do. How could he baptize the Messiah, the Christ?

The apostle Matthew records John trying to prevent Jesus, saying, "I need to be baptized by You, and are You coming to me?" (Matt. 3:14).

That's when Jesus put everything in perspective for John. "Permit it to be so now, for thus it is fitting for us to fulfill all righteousness" (v. 15).

By saying His baptism would be "fulfilling all righteousness," Jesus was acknowledging that preparations had been made for Him to be baptized. It was part of a master plan that was prepared long before Jesus walked into the Jordan River that day.

The Scriptures describe, in advance, the details of His birth, including the place, those who would come to worship Him, those who would try to kill Him, where His family would flee to, and who His family would be—the family of David into which He would be born.

The Scriptures describe how He would die, the details of His betrayal by Judas, Peter's denial, His torture, and His last words on the cross.

The Scriptures also detail the preparations made for the Holy Spirit to empower Him, for the Word of God to be His truth document, and for the disciples who would serve with Him.

The Bible tells us John the Baptist himself came to prepare the way for Jesus. In addition, John's ministry was also prepared for by the prophet Isaiah, who said, "The voice of one crying in the wilderness: 'Prepare the way of the LORD; Make straight in the desert a highway for our God'" (Isa. 40:3).

Just as God made preparations for Jesus long before He came into the world, so God has made preparations for the great works He has planned for you to do as well.

HELP *Wanted*

Throughout the world, 443,000 Christian missionaries in 4,340 agencies currently are deployed to countries outside their own.[1]

"Blessed be the God and Father of our Lord Jesus Christ, who has blessed us with every spiritual blessing in the heavenly places in Christ, just as He chose us in Him before the foundation of the world" (Eph. 1:3–4).

Every possible spiritual advantage God could set aside for you, He did. He had your name placed on the plan long before even your great-great-great-grandparents were born. For one simple purpose: to prepare you to do something to make your life count.

....

More of a Marriott woman than the "me-Tarzan-you-Jane" type, Donna would be the first to tell you that a bamboo hut with no electricity or running water was not her first choice for a home.

Now, on top of that, Islamic rebels? *I don't think so.*

Yet, as Donna and Bill talked and prayed about it, they realized it came down to something their beloved pastor back home always said. "Do not doubt in the dark what God has shown you in the light." Donna and Bill were certain God had led them in "the light" to the jungle. That was further confirmed a few years later.

Bill was teaching an overview of the Bible when one old man, a clan leader from the southern part of the island, showed up. He was not a Christian. He listened, and at the end, he did what polite Palawanos do to show they have paid attention: he summarized the whole message out loud.

He really got it, Bill thought.

Two years later, this man's wife, a little old Palawano granny, visited Bill and Donna on their porch.

"You know," the woman casually commented in her native language, "the only reason my family listened to you was because of what my father said when I was a child."

Bill asked what she meant.

The Palawano woman told them that her father had been a type of prophet in the tribe, a high-level spiritual leader. When she was a child, which would have been before World War II, her dad had sat her and her siblings and cousins down and told them something.

"Someday, Americans will come with a book," he said. "They will live among the Palawanos and tell us how to know God and have eternal life. This will be the truth and you should believe it."

When Bill and Donna first came to the valley and began teaching, the granny heard about it and kept nagging her husband: "Go see what the Americans are teaching. Maybe this is what my dad told us about."

The Palawano man eventually went. He was the old man who "got it." Both he and his wife became believers.

....

God was preparing the ministry on Palawan long before Bill and Donna were born. God also knew that the rebels would show up at Donna's door. He knew she would be in the house alone with little kids. He knew she was not completely comfortable with living in the jungle and would want to go back to San Diego. So, to keep them on course, he prepared Bill and Donna's pastor to teach the key principle of believing what you've learned in the light, even when you're in the dark.

Bill and Donna have been on Palawan for twenty-eight years. The rebels left them alone, and they have planted several churches. They also are close to finishing the translation of the New Testament into the indigenous language.

You and I are not messiahs, of course, but just as Jesus came to do something to love this world, we too have a mandate to do something loving and, in our own small way, to bring hope to someone who is hopeless. Just as God made all the necessary preparations for Jesus to accomplish His purpose, He has done the same for our success as well.

Jesus needed only three years to make an impact on the world. And it was an impact that is still going strong almost two thousand years later. This was not only because He was so well prepared but because He did something about those preparations.

He took advantage of them.

The stakes are high. God has eternally prepared you to do something significant in someone's life. In part 2 you will gain insights on how God has made preparations for you to make your life count.

Don't waste another minute.

ACTIVITIES

Identify one skill that you have been prepared with, which could not have come from anyone but God. Then with that skill in mind, write down one type of person you might think He prepared you to help.

Dear Lord, please give me eyes to see the preparations You have made for me. Please give me the faith to believe that what I think are coincidences might actually be the advance work of Your hand.

HEROES

Find out more about Donna and Bill at www.milesmcpherson.com.

2

Romeo

Purpose—Obedience

Jesus answered and said to him, "If anyone loves Me, he will keep My word; and My Father will love him, and We will come to him and make Our home with him."

—John 14:23

"We have Sheri on the line," the radio DJ announced. "Sheri, are you there?"

"Yes, I'm here. Hi—" Sheri said. It felt weird talking into her telephone and hearing her voice come out her radio a split second later. She turned the stereo off.

"Welcome to the 'War of the Roses,' Sheri! How are you today?"

"Fine . . . I think." She sighed. She didn't feel like admitting her heart was breaking.

"So, tell us what's going on with—is it your husband?"

"Yes, my husband. Romeo. We've been married for six months, and, uh, I think he may be cheating on me."

"Ah, that's rotten, Sheri. Tell us why you think that."

"Well . . . ," she took a deep breath, "when we first met, we spent every day together. We'd do stuff like walking around the park every Saturday, holding hands, talking about everything, especially how we looked forward to having a family together. He was always telling me he loved me. He was like my best friend . . ."

"Then what happened?" the radio host interjected.

"About two months ago, he started telling me he had to work late on Friday evenings, and on Saturday mornings he was too tired to walk."

"Is that the only thing that changed?" the DJ asked.

Sheri felt herself start to get teary. "No. I found lipstick on a shirt in the bag he was taking to the cleaners. It wasn't mine."

"Uh-oh," the DJ groaned.

"There's more—" Sheri whispered, sniffling. "Someone keeps calling the house, but when I answer the phone, they hang up. Last Saturday, Romeo slept in again, and that night the phone rang. I picked up, and again the caller hung up on me. Five minutes later, he left the house and did not come back for three hours."

The DJ made sympathetic sounds and then said, "Listen, we can help you get to the bottom of this. We'll have Joe call Romeo, and offer to send a dozen roses from him to anyone he wants, free. Hopefully he will send them to you. You want us to do that, Sheri?"

Sniffling and taking a deep breath, Sheri said, "Okay."

"You sure you're ready for this, no matter what happens?" asked the DJ.

Sheri didn't hesitate. "Yes. I need to know."

"Okay, Sheri, then let's get Romeo on the line."

Sheri heard a dial tone, the faint beeps of a number being dialed, and a half-dozen rings. Then—

"Hello?"

She recognized Romeo's voice.

"Hello. Is this Romeo?" Joe said.

"Yeah, who's this?"

"Hi, Romeo. My name is Joe. I'm calling from Truly Yours, a new flower shop that has just opened in your neighborhood. We're offering you a free dozen roses you can send to whomever you want. No strings. Just a way to introduce ourselves to the community."

"Did you say free?" Romeo sounded suspicious.

"Right. No charge—"

"What's the catch?" Romeo demanded.

"No catch at all, Romeo. You can send the free roses to whoever you want. All we need is a name, an address, and something to go on the card. That's it. Do you wanna do it?"

"Free?"

"Yup!"

"Okay, I'll do it."

"Great! What name would you like to put on the card?" Joe asked.

"Uh—"

Sheri bit her lip.

"Laurie . . ."

She sucked in her breath.

"Okay now, what would you like to say on the card?"

"How about, *Saturday was amazing. Can't wait to see you this weekend*—"

Sheri couldn't hold it in any longer. "Romeo! How could you!" she screamed into the phone. "*Who's Laurie!?*"

"Sheri? Is that you? What's going on?"

"That's what I'd like to know! Who is Laurie? Who are you cheating on me with?"

Sheri flashed back to their wedding ceremony, with the vows and promises, and felt her life crumbling around her. She thought of all the intimate moments in which she felt vulnerable but protected, safe in his arms.

"She's nothing!" Romeo stuttered to explain. "Just someone I met at the bar the other night—"

"You're lying!"

"She means nothing to me! Sheri, what are you doing? This is stupid! You know I love you—"

• •

Jesus stood surrounded by men in religious robes and multicolored turbans. They were taking turns questioning Him, like tag-team wrestling.

First the Sadducees confronted Jesus about the resurrection. They were "sad, you see," because they did not believe in it.

After Jesus bent their minds with His wisdom, they walked away with their tails between their legs and tagged the Pharisees, who jumped into the ring for a shot at Jesus.

Jesus must have rolled His eyes when one of the Pharisees challenged Him with an *Are You Smarter than a 5th Grader?* question. "Teacher, which is the great commandment in the law?"

God's purpose for your life is to love Him by obeying Him.

He answered, "'You shall love the LORD your God with all your heart, with all your soul, and with all your mind.' This is the first and great commandment. And the second is like it: 'You shall love your neighbor as yourself.' On these two commandments hang all the Law and the Prophets" (Matt. 22:36–40).

What is the fastest way of being blessed by God? That is easy: keep the great commandment to love God and love your neighbor.

Loving the world was undoubtedly the purpose of Jesus' life. You know the familiar Bible verse: "For God so loved the world that He gave His only begotten Son . . ." (John 3:16). This is also the purpose of our lives. In other words, the foundation of everything we do must be out of loving God and loving our neighbor. Jesus also told us that people would know we were His disciples by our love, one for another (John 13:35).

· ·

If Romeo loved Sheri, as he claimed, why did he find himself on the radio program getting slammed by her?

Let me tell you why. Romeo did not know that love has rules. Or, if he did, he ignored them.

Loving God is not some emotionally based, do-gooder kind of thing. No, it is very specific and simple. To love God is to *obey God*.

First John 5:3 says, "For this is the love of God, that we keep His commandments."

The main rule for loving is to obey God.

That's it.

Because the second commandment, loving your neighbor as yourself, is an extension of the first, its definition is also pretty simple. If loving God is obeying His commandments, loving someone else is helping them obey God.

When Romeo saw the Laurie lady in the bar, his hormones screamed, *Check it out! You want to kiss her, don't you? Correction: you need to kiss her! Go, man, go!*

At that point Romeo should have expressed love toward his wife and walked out of the bar.

Love does not have an emotional "opt out" clause that says, *I can obey when I feel like it.* No, love is a commitment, not an emotion. There will be times when our mood—or emotional condition, or physical will—does not want to obey God. But that is just too bad. If we really love someone, we will do whatever we can to stay true to that love. Period. End of story. That is the greatest commandment. That is our God-given purpose.

Jesus gave His life, not because of some emotional attachment to someone or something, but out of obedience. His obedience led Him into the desert to be tempted by the devil. His obedience is what led to all of His miracles. His obedience paved the way for our sins to be forgiven.

He humbled Himself and died on the cross out of obedience (Phil. 2:3–8).

His obedient act is what makes our obedient acts possible.

God's purpose for your life is to love Him by obeying Him. He has created you to do something great with your life. Each of us will have unique things to do, but whatever we *do*, it should be out of obedience to God.

In part 3 of this book, you will glean five insights from Jesus on how to fulfill your purpose of loving God through humble obedience.

ACTIVITIES

Identify one area of your life that you know is disobedient to God. Now write down the first step you can take to bring this area of your life back into obedience.

I will obey God by _____

_____

_____

Dear Lord, I want to love You with all of my heart. Please reveal to me those areas of my life that are disobedient to You, Lord. Please give me clear direction through Your Word, other people, or that still small voice in my heart, on how to bring my life into obedience to You.

3

Coach

Pain—It Doesn't Have to Only Hurt

Where do wars and fights come from among you? Do they not come from your desires for pleasure that war in your members?

—James 4:1

The phone rang as my wife, Debbie, and I were packing for a long weekend in Palm Springs. My position coach was on the phone.

"Miles, I got some bad news for you."

I was entering my fifth season as a defensive back with the San Diego Chargers and our minicamp was only a few weeks away. Minicamp is a springtime training camp that lasts about four days, and usually takes place immediately after the college draft.

Bad news? Am I getting cut? It wouldn't be the first time.

Six weeks before the regular season, NFL training camps typically begin with about a hundred players, and on average nine of them get cut each week. Being cut means you get fired—with no notice, no severance, no warm fuzzies. Your contract is torn up and canceled.

With the average career being less than four years, NFL actually means Not For Long.

Still, watching guys get cut is not a pretty sight. Coaches usually try to inform the players when no one is around. Next thing you know, you see players dressed in street clothes, occasionally in tears, giving handshakes and hugs to the players in their uniforms.

But it doesn't always work out that way. Sometimes players are notified while walking into the locker room before practice, or pulled out of meetings, or even grabbed while their feet are getting taped.

The first time I got cut, I cried.

I was a rookie with the Los Angeles Rams lying on the bed in my hotel room. It was the day of the last cut down to fifty-three guys. I heard a knock on the door. I jumped up, stood at the door, took a deep breath as my heart raced. I braced myself for the bad news and opened the door.

"*Hola. Cómo está usted?* Do you need maid service?"

The lady's hair blew back as I exhaled a typhoon of relief. "No, thank you!" I paused for a second, and then slammed the door.

Thirty minutes later, as I was walking over to the locker room, the strength coach told me to go see the general manager.

As slowly as I could, I walked past the field on my way to the GM's office, thinking, *I belong out there. I know the plays. I can do this.* This could be my last few moments in the NFL, and maybe in California.

Do I go back to the University of New Haven and engineering school? No way.

Do I go back home to New York then? And do what?

I am a football player, I just need a team.

Sure enough, the GM told me I had been released. But he said to come back the next day, for what I did not know.

Back in my hotel room, I just lay down and cried. I didn't know what I was going to do.

The next day, I walked into the GM's office, expecting nothing but a plane ticket home.

The GM was grinning.

There's nothing funny about this, brother. What are you smiling about?

But all of a sudden, there was hope. They wanted to pay to keep me in town just in case someone on the team got hurt.

Nine weeks later I signed with the San Diego Chargers.

The second time I was cut, there was no smiling GM. My coach caught me in the locker room and asked for my playbook. It came during the season after I had made the team, in my fourth year with the Chargers. Debbie was seven months pregnant with our first child. We had just bought our first home, and to make things worse, it was the day before I qualified for the NFL retirement plan. Yes, the day before.

I got a part-time job and went back to school. Five weeks later, the Chargers asked me to rejoin the team for the remainder of the season. We also had a healthy baby girl.

Now, a third time? *Am I getting cut again?* And oh yeah, we had a strong suspicion Debbie was pregnant.

....

The crowd parted. A slick, rich lawyer type wearing a first-century Armani suit pimp-walked toward Jesus. With a sly grin, he spoke loud enough for the crowd to hear. "Good teacher, what good thing do I need to do to go to heaven?"

Every head in the crowd turned to see what Jesus would say.

Jesus looked at the wealthy young man for a moment, and then said something like this: "If you call Me good, then you need to call Me God. And if you want to enter into eternal life, you need to keep the commandments."

Now "Big Daddy" really started smiling. He may have been stuck on himself, but he did know Old Testament law. He bounced back with, "Which ones?"

This guy wasn't dumb. He wouldn't ask these questions in front of all of these people if he weren't confident he had the right answers. His reputation was on the line.

Well, Jesus was smart too. In fact, being God, He knew everything about the pretty-boy law expert

HELP *Wanted*

In 2008, 2.6 million people in the United States lost their jobs.[2]

and his game of justifying himself. He knew where the man was heading, but he gave him the expected answer anyway.

"Do not murder, commit adultery, steal, or lie; honor your parents; and love your neighbor as yourself . . ."

The young man extended his arms, palms up, and looked at the crowd on his right and left. "Just as I thought! I am going to heaven. Thank you, Jesus, for clarifying that to everyone in the listening audience—"

"Not so fast, fella," Jesus said (I'm paraphrasing here!), interrupting his "I'm heaven-bound" party. "If you really want to be perfect, sell all that you have and give it to the poor, and you will have treasure in heaven. Then come follow Me."

The lawyer's smile dropped like a brick. *Give up my Benz?* he thought. *Sell my flat screens? Live in an apartment? You want me to shop where?*

The crowd started to buzz. For once speechless, the rich young man turned and disappeared into the crowd. (See Luke 18:18–32.)

> However you look at it, pain will always be part of our lives, but it can do more than just hurt.

Pain is inevitable in our lives. Sometimes it is physical, other times emotional. It results from living in a broken world. It can be caused by persecution, gossip, being betrayed, dumb things we do to ourselves, or even standing up for God.

However you look at it, pain will always be part of our lives, but it can do more than just hurt.

In every painful situation we will face, God gives us an opportunity to trust that He will not only get us through it but help us nurture a deeper trust in Him through it.

Faced with that call from my coach, I had to reconcile my dreams with the belief that something good could come from getting cut from the Chargers.

I needed to realize that pain can do more than just hurt.

It took God three times to get the message through my thick head, but I finally figured it out.

The first time I was cut, I was *sad*. Completely lost and clueless, I cried.

The second time I got cut, I was *mad*. I felt like it was maliciously done after I made the team.

Yes, this was my third time, but instead of being sad or mad, I was *glad*. Why? Because I had learned to trust that God had a plan.

Even when people do hurtful things to you, God has a plan to turn the experiences into something positive in your life. In some cases you might not see the plan for a long time, or ever. But rest assured it's there, because a loving God is in control. God always takes care of us.

The sting of pain is way overrated. Fear is caused by an expectation of something undesirable happening. But if we think about it, once we get through the painful experience, we often find ourselves stronger and closer to God.

The rich young lawyer couldn't trust God beyond losing his stuff—he couldn't imagine God could provide something better for him. He was ignorant of the blessings on the other side of his painful separation from his status symbols. Consequently he walked away sorrowful.

God was so faithful the previous two times I was cut, I was confident He had something prepared for me beyond this third time. From a human perspective I was losing my job. From God's perspective I was moving on to my next assignment.

God had made that fact so clear to me that I was able to say goodbye without bitterness to my head coach, Don Coryell, one of the best football coaches of all time. Not only that, because of his sweet nature and our good relationship, I could place my arm around him and pray for him before I walked out of the stadium for the last time.

I had made a decision to want what God wanted, not what I wanted.

If you don't want pain merely to hurt, do something *and trust that God knows what He is doing*. In part 4 you will learn five ways God can help you turn pain into something powerful in your life. Pain can do more than hurt.

By the way, after I learned I was cut, I hung up the phone and went on to have a great time in Palm Springs. And oh yeah, my wife *was* pregnant.

ACTIVITIES

Think of the last time you were in a painful predicament and identify one positive lesson that came out of it.

Share that lesson with someone today and be blessed.

Dear Lord, thank You for faithfully bringing me through my trials. Thank You for the lessons You have taught me. Please bring a hurting person into my life today whom I can bless with my story of trust.

Hear NFL players talk about getting cut at www.milesmcpherson.com.

4

Greg and Cindy

Power—The Ability to Do

Now to Him who is able to do exceedingly abundantly above all that
we ask or think, according to the power that works in us, to Him
be glory in the church by Christ Jesus to all generations, forever and
ever. Amen.

—Ephesians 3:20–21

Three of my senior staff and I sat frozen at the boardroom table. I
think our mouths were hanging open too. The voice in my head was
screaming, *What did this guy just say?*

At the end of the table, the fund-raising consultant for the building project tapped his finger on the financial reports. "You need
$8.3 million in four months—and based on the financial analysis,
you do not have anyone in Rock Church with that kind of money,"
he said.

The average age of the people who attended our church was
twenty-nine years old, so I knew he was probably right.

It had been four years since we found the 244,000-square-foot
building we wanted to transform into a church and school complex. It

was just about one and a half times the length of a football field—444 feet long—and 45 feet high. The size of Noah's ark, actually.

Formerly a school on a naval base designed to train people for human wars, the building was going to become a place to train people for God's spiritual battles. We planned to demolish half the structure and construct a 3,500-seat sanctuary. It would be divided into sixty-six sections, one for every book in the Bible, with every seat labeled with a verse. We envisioned a 3,600-square-foot high-definition video experience, twenty-four prayer niches, a Holy of Holies–sized area for people to walk into at altar calls. The other half would be transformed into offices, a full-service bookstore and café, and a state-of-the-art K–12 school.

For almost four years, we had been raising money, securing financing, getting permits, designing the building, and promoting the project from the pulpit. We had been showing the congregation architectural drawings and casting a vision for how we would use the building to evangelize San Diego County and the world. With dozens of contractors lined up and the publicity plan in place, everything pointed to a close of escrow on September 15, with construction starting thirty days later. The clock was ticking.

Now everything was in jeopardy. The delay of the $7.2 million pledge had backed us into a corner.

Our regular monthly financial update to the congregation was scheduled for the upcoming Sunday. We had only four months to go before the bank needed money—not prayer or Bible verses. The consultant, relying on his financial analysis and best practices from years of experience, gave me clear instructions.

"Ask only for $1.1 million. Even though you need $8.3 million, assume you will get the $7.2 million pledge and tell the church you need $1.1 million," he said. "You don't want to discourage your congregation by asking for $8.3 million with only four months to go."

He looked me in the eye. "Trust me. Put a full court press on the $7.2 million pledge and get the remaining $1.1 million from the church. That's all they can afford."

• •

The tan stone pillars holding up the rock slab ceiling of Pontius Pilate's basement meeting hall were all that stood between a bloodied

Jesus and three hundred Roman soldiers. In their golden helmets and crimson robes, the warriors surrounded the beaten Savior while Pontius Pilate interrogated Him.

Outside, the angry crowd screamed, "Crucify Him! Crucify Him!"

Pilate, the Roman governor, was under pressure by the Jewish leaders to execute Jesus because He claimed to be God.

As his soldiers snickered at the man they viewed as a pitiful, helpless, fake king of the Jews, Pilate slowly strutted around Him.

"Are You not speaking to me?" he demanded. "Do You not know that I have power to crucify You, and power to release You?" (John 19:10).

The ultimate power one man can have over another is the right to legally kill him. Pilate did have that authority over Jesus. But for some reason, the "fake" king of the Jews didn't seem bothered. Instead, Jesus answered, "You could have no power at all against Me unless it had been given you from above" (John 19:11).

Pilate did not understand there were two kinds of power, and both were given by God. He possessed a vast amount of earthly power in the form of judicial authority, ability, and opportunity to crucify people. But it was limited to the natural world. Pilate could kill Jesus' body. But he could not keep Jesus in the grave (Matt. 10:28).

Jesus had a superior form of power. His was spiritual power—something Pilate knew nothing about. Spiritual power can reach down into the physical world and reverse anything natural power has done. Jesus had, and still has, the authority, ability, and opportunity to do anything He wants; He can overcome natural power if He wants to.

This power is based solely on one's relationship with God. It is given by God on an individual basis.

Walking up behind Jesus, whose body was trembling and bleeding, Pilate asked, "Are You the King of the Jews?" (John 18:33).

Basically he was asking, *If You are a king, where is Your kingdom? Where is Your power? Why couldn't You prevent Yourself from being arrested and treated like this, by the people whom You are supposed to be king over? Help me understand all of this, Jesus.*

Jesus was from another kingdom and possessed a different kind of super power. In John 18:36 He said, "My kingdom is not of this world. If My kingdom were of this world, My servants would fight, so that I should not be delivered to the Jews; but now My kingdom is not from here."

The problem with our financial consultant's recommendation was that it did not consider the possibility of a miracle. But then again, his job was to advise us based on the numbers. Our responsibility was to act on faith in what we believed God could and would do. He could intervene spiritually into our natural situation if He wanted to.

If God backed us into a corner, all we could do was be obedient and trust that He would get us out of there and back into the center of the ring.

Jesus had access to spiritual power—authority, ability, and opportunity to even overcome death. That was the reason He wasn't worried about Pilate's threat to crucify Him.

It is also the reason I told the church we needed $8.3 million. I said that we needed a minimum of $1.1 million. But I explained that a $7.2 million pledge was in jeopardy, and if it fell through, we actually needed $8.3 million.

Just as Jesus' power could reverse a death sentence, God could reach down into our circumstance and get us the money we needed.

If you're going to do works greater than Jesus, just as He promised you could, then you need spiritual power.

There is no way you will be able to fulfill your spiritual purpose without it.

. . . .

After the service that next Sunday, in which I announced our financial needs, a 6-foot-2, 220-pound baldheaded stranger with a goatee, wearing shorts and a T-shirt, tapped me on the shoulder. He told me he wanted to talk about funding the building. Even though I'd heard offers like that before that didn't pan out, I agreed to meet.

A week later I met with Greg and his wife, Cindy. They were new to the Rock and had not been included in our financial analysis. In fact, they lived five hours away and flew down regularly—in their own plane—to visit their daughter, who attended the Rock while studying at a college in town.

They told me that in one of our services the Lord told them to help the church with the $1.1 million. Two days later a broker approached them, offering to sell part of Greg's business, which he eventually did.

God's powerful hand was reaching down from the spiritual world into our physical world and stirring things up.

A few months later, on September 4, their sale was complete. On September 10, Greg, Cindy, and their daughter, Rebekah, flew to San Diego in their plane, sat across from me at a table in a restaurant, and leaned a $5.5 million check against the saltshaker.

I picked up that check about ten times during lunch. I needed to assure myself it was real. I kept telling myself that God had really answered our prayers.

Soon after that, by taking a second look at all our financing and receiving an additional $1 million in gifts, we were able to close escrow. The $7.2 million pledge never came through, but God helped us begin construction on time anyway.

Not only does God own cattle on a thousand hills, He owns the thousand hills as well (Ps. 50:10). God has resources you do not know about.

> **Most of all, God has a desire to bless you with spiritual power from heaven—the authority, ability, and opportunity to do something beyond your imagination.**

He has timing you do not know about.

He has ideas and thoughts that are as high above our heads as the heavens themselves (Isa. 55:9).

He can turn the hearts of human beings like rivers of water.

Most of all, God has a desire to bless you with spiritual power from heaven—the authority, ability, and opportunity to do something beyond your imagination.

Not only did Jesus promise we would do greater works than He did, He also prepared us with the tools necessary for us to do those works. One of those tools is spiritual power.

In part 5, you will gain five insights into how to maximize the power of God in your life and how to utilize that power to do something of eternal significance.

ACTIVITIES

Identify a dilemma in your life that requires the powerful hand of God. Acknowledge to Him your need for His intervention, and then walk into it by faith, confident that He will act on your behalf. Record in writing what He does on your behalf to honor your faith.

Dear Lord, I acknowledge that I alone am powerless to do the things You want me to do. Please intervene in my life, especially the situation I have identified above. Please open the eyes of my heart that I may see Your power at work in my life.

HEROES

Hear Greg and Cindy talk about the process of giving their gift at www.milesmcpherson.com.

5

Brian and Haley

Passion—Never Give Up

But Jesus said to him, "No one, having put his hand to the plow, and looking back, is fit for the kingdom of God."

— Luke 9:62

Brian rubbed his hands toward the orange flames that flickered above the rim of the black 25-gallon barrel. It was the day after Christmas, and his grease-covered overalls were barely keeping the nineteen-year-old warm. On a lunch break at the Oregon tree farm where he was learning forestry, he was thinking of his fiancée, Haley. That warmed up his heart as he faced the fire.

The flames began to shoot higher than his head. Brian reached behind for a bucket of water to dump into the barrel. He swung the pail over his shoulder. As the fluid started to pour out, he smelled too late that it wasn't water. It was gasoline.

A ball of flame the size of a car swallowed him. He turned into a twirling torch. Flapping his arms, he threw himself on the ground. But it was gravel and did nothing to squelch the blaze.

His boss ran over and threw a fire blanket on him, but his grease-soaked clothing kept burning. He pulled off Brian's clothes, carried him to a van, and drove his smoldering black and pink body twenty miles to the nearest hospital. On the way, Brian's swelling throat began to choke him.

The fire had cooked him. With third-degree burns over 97 percent of his body, Brian's doctors gave him a one-in-a-thousand chance of survival.

He spent his first month in a coma. When he woke up, he realized he was blind. He asked his mother, "How bad were my hands burned?" She told him they had to cut off his arms just below the elbows to save him from infection. He then asked, "What about my legs?" She told him they had to cut off his right forefoot and his left leg just below the knee.

Gone also were his dark, athletic good looks, and the future Haley and he had dreamed of, building a cabin together, camping and hiking. Perhaps gone also was the chance of having the family they wanted.

Now Brian wondered, was Haley gone too?

• •

Blood and pieces of flesh dribbled into the dirt as Jesus' shredded body dangled on the cross.

Trash-talkers in the crowd mocked Him from below.

Ha! You said You had the power to rise from the dead, they yelled. *Why can't You even come down from that cross? For that matter, how come You couldn't stop them from crucifying You in the first place? Hypocrite!*

Claiming to be a savior, He was crucified as a common criminal. *Save Yourself—and us!* sneered one of the robbers crucified with Him.

Jesus' critics felt vindicated. Here was proof that this guy was a con man. And His disciples' confidence had sunk to virtually nothing. The blood of their teacher, Messiah, and savior was splattering the crowd below as the wind blew over His mangled body. In their minds, Jesus was one miracle short.

Jesus had been falsely accused, unjustly tried in court, maliciously beaten and crucified. He also would soon become the very evil that caused His death, a death designed to pay the price of forgiveness for that evil—sin.

Jesus, who had no sin, would literally become sin (2 Cor. 5:21). Hanging on that cross, Jesus was drowning in a suffocating quicksand of spiritual darkness. He felt so distant from His Father God that He cried out, *"Eloi, Eloi, lama sabachthani?"* which is translated, "My God, My God, why have You forsaken Me?" (Mark 15:34).

But even though Christ felt abandoned and forsaken by His Father, He remained obedient.

At any time He could have given up and pulled the plug on the whole process. Yet Jesus never quit on us.

Haley's heart-shaped face was tense and sad as she stared down at what was left of her fiancé, unconscious and wrapped in bandages.

She was thinking back. They had started dating when she was sixteen and he was seventeen. A year later, he had proposed on one knee at the Jesus Northwest festival in Vancouver, Washington, telling her he wanted to care for her the rest of her life. She had thrown her hands over her mouth and laughed out loud with excitement. "Yes! I will marry you!"

She had had no idea what she was committing to. All she knew was that she was in love and wanted to spend the rest of her life with this funny, hardworking, and good-looking Christian man.

But now every physical attribute she was attracted to was replaced by one blanket of scar tissue. No arms, no ears, one and a half legs, and half a foot. Did her commitment include being married to a guy who would never hold her the way he had? Who, even if he could have kids, would never see them—or her—again?

Brian himself gave her an opportunity to walk away.

"I'll understand if you do not want to go through with the wedding, Haley," he said during one of her many visits to the hospital. "You did not sign up for this."

Could she be expected to stick to her commitment? After all, she was only eighteen.

When we make a commitment to love or obey God, it is not conditional on it being easy. It is our job to love and obey Him. It is up to Him to decide under what conditions we will be asked to obey.

43

Our lives will go through unexpected ups and downs. Our job is to simply hold on to God by consistently obeying Him.

Life comes with unexpected tragedies, and they can be tough. No doubt about it.

Figuratively speaking, you will be burned and even have your legs cut out from under you at times. You will be betrayed by people you thought were your friends. There is simply no avoiding it. But if you are going to do something to make your life count, there will be times when your passion will need to push through your pain.

If you want to make your life count, learn to take an "eight count."

Just as in Brian and Haley's life, we can feel overmatched at times—especially if we try to do life without God. There will be other times when God tells us to get out of the battle. Walking away from a responsibility that God wants us to push through is not an option. God's commitment to us is to never leave nor forsake us, no matter how tough the battle gets. Our commitment to Him must be to trust Him and to fight, even if He sends us a challenge that most would walk away from.

Winning the battles we face in life is not our responsibility. Obeying God by faith is. The outcome is completely up to Him.

Meanwhile, Satan will do everything he can to get us to give up. The devil will try to convince us to walk away.

Don't believe him. You cannot do something with your life if you walk away from tough situations before God tells you to.

Thank God Jesus didn't quit.

• •

Haley did not quit on Brian. Haley had made a promise to love him, even into the difficult unknown. After all, what she was actually in love with was not affected by the fire.

When the going gets tough, it is your passion that keeps you going. Your passion is what pushes you through the unknown, the difficult times. If someone tells passion to stop fighting, passion says no.

Without the passion to do something, you will never complete your God-given mission.

44

As you're serving the Lord, how far into difficult situations are you willing to push before quitting? Are you willing to trust God through thick and thin?

What will you do when everyone around you is suggesting, "You don't need to go through with this"?

If you want to make your life count, learn to take an "eight count."

An eight count is when a referee in a boxing match counts to eight to see if a boxer can continue fighting. It comes after the fighter gets up from a "ten count" and still looks a little wobbly.

The next time you feel like *I don't want to be embarrassed*, give yourself an eight count. When you think, *I don't want to get ridiculed, I don't want to give up my Saturday*, or *I don't want to give my hard-earned money away*, stop, and ask yourself, "Where would I be if my Lord quit?"

Then take your eight count by reciting eight words:

I will not quit, because He didn't quit.

It is time to get up and do something.

The last section of this book, what we'll call your Passion Week, will guide you through five lessons taught to us by Jesus through His Passion Week.

My prayer is that you would not quit interacting with this book until you are completely finished reading it and doing everything that God challenges you to do through your reading.

ACTIVITIES

Memorize your "eight count"—*I will not quit, because He didn't quit*—by reciting it eight consecutive times at least three different times today.

Dear Lord, the next time I am challenged, or tempted to take a shortcut in obeying You, please prompt me to take an eight count. I want my commitment to You to be full of passion. Dear Lord, just as You are committed to complete the work You started in me, I want to be committed to let You finish that work (Phil. 1:6).

HEROES

Meet Brian and Haley Sakultarawattn (pronounced skoon-tra-WATT) and their kids at www.miles mcpherson.com.

DO Something! Myth 1

If I am scared to do something,
God must not want me to do it.

The Lies Behind It

- Our feelings should tell us what to do.
- God can't use scared people.
- We should never do anything we are afraid of.
- Being uncomfortable goes against God's desire for our lives.

The Truth

- We should expect to be challenged by God.
- God has the power to overcome our feelings and hesitations,
- and He can move powerfully in spite of our weakness.

Scripture

There is no fear in love. But perfect love drives out fear, because fear has to do with punishment. The one who fears is not made perfect in love.

—1 John 4:18 NIV

Something to Remember

It's important to recognize your feelings but not be controlled by them. Let go of your fear and God will use you for mighty things.

Part 2

Preparation

Advance Work

Before you were born, God made **preparations** for you to live a significant life. He provided you with all the tools, both natural and supernatural, and the opportunities you would need to do something of eternal significance.

> For we are His workmanship, created in Christ Jesus for good works, which God prepared beforehand that we should walk in them.
>
> — Ephesians 2:10

6

Vince and Vanessa

The Resurrection of Faith

So the Lord said, "If you have faith as a mustard seed, you can say to this mulberry tree, 'Be pulled up by the roots and be planted in the sea,' and it would obey you."

—Luke 17:6

"Honey, we can work this out."

Vince felt Vanessa reach up and wrap her arms around his muscular shoulders. He bunched his dark eyebrows together and clinched his eyes shut against the tears he didn't want his wife to see.

"No." He ran thick fingers through his dark brown hair, and sat up on the edge of Vanessa's sofa.

Vince and Vanessa had met while working at a gym in Southern California. He was a 6-foot-5, 240-pound personal trainer from New Jersey. She was a blonde Pilates instructor with an ear-to-ear "I-love-everyone-I-know" smile.

"Vince," Vanessa began again, wiping mascara from the corners of her eyes. "Just like Pastor Miles said, we never should have moved to Jersey and tried to start a business right after we got married.

51

You were never around. Leaving California was hard for me. I didn't have any friends, and I had to work two jobs. And living with your parents—"

Vince glared at Vanessa and she stopped. He knew how hopeful she was that they would get back together, even though she had moved out and returned to San Diego to get away from their drama. But he didn't want to hear any of that now. They'd been fighting for months before she had left him, and during every visit he had made to San Diego, the tension was thick.

"No, Vanessa. It's not going to work out. I can't do this."

A week later he put divorce papers in the mail. The marriage was basically over. But something mysterious happened between Vince's and Vanessa's mailboxes.

....

The crowd was pushing Jesus left and right like bumper cars as He steered His way to Jairus's house. He and His disciples had just crossed the Sea of Galilee, where people had mobbed them, seeking hope for their hopeless situations. One of them was Jairus, an important leader of the local synagogue. Jairus had shoved his way forward to fall at Jesus' feet and beg for a miracle.

"My little girl is dying. Please. Come and heal her. Hurry!"

Without a word Jesus followed the desperate father as he rushed toward home where his beloved twelve-year-old daughter lay surrounded by family and friends. But as they were making their way, they were met by bad news. "Some came from the ruler of the synagogue's house who said, 'Your daughter is dead. Why trouble the Teacher any further?'" (Mark 5:35).

Jesus looked at the messenger, then at Jairus. Then He said, "Don't be afraid, only believe."

Have faith.

....

"Miles, I can't do it. It's not going to work."

I could hear depression and confusion in Vince's voice on the phone. I had become friends with Vanessa and Vince while working out at their gym before their move to New Jersey. I invited them to visit the Rock Church. Eventually they came, and committed their lives to Jesus Christ. I had the honor of doing their wedding.

After Vanessa returned to San Diego, she was ready to get serious with God and place the fate of her failing marriage in His hands.

Vince, though, was running from God. His new athletic training facility in New Jersey was open and business was booming. Some of his friends were telling him to give up on his marriage and get on with his life, and he was thinking about it.

But one night he called me. Over and over again he kept telling me that getting back together wouldn't work. "I know I'm still married to Vanessa, Miles, but I can't do it. What would happen if we had a baby? Or if we had financial problems? We would just fight again and she'd just go back to California. I can't do it. I just can't."

"So why did you call me?" I asked. He knew what I would say. I had said it a million times. *Have faith.*

He paused. "I don't know. But I just don't feel anything anymore."

"This had nothing to do with feeling," I told him. "Vince, when you married Vanessa, you made a vow to God. You need to make fixing this marriage your first priority, not because you feel like it, but because it is right in the eyes of God."

Jesus Himself said, "Have you not read that He who made them at the beginning 'made them male and female,' and said, 'For this reason a man shall leave his father and mother and be joined to his wife, and the two shall become one flesh'? So then, they are no longer two but one flesh. Therefore what God has joined together, let not man separate" (Matt. 19:4–6).

There are, unfortunately, some marriages that need to come to an end, but Vince's situation was not one of them.

Vince needed to trust that God would honor his faithful obedience. Faith is based not on feelings but fact. The feelings would *follow* his faith.

• •

Faith is the substance of things hoped for and the evidence of things not seen (Heb. 11:1). Faith enables us to pursue something tangible while relying on something invisible to help us get it.

From the beginning, God not only prepared faith for you and me to use, He made us creatures of faith. We exercise faith all day long.

Think about it. Every time you breathe, you trust the fact that oxygen—something you have never seen—will fill your lungs and keep you alive. You don't choose air over propane gas only because you feel like it but because oxygen is the only thing that works. You base your faith on a fact.

Same thing with gravity. You respect the fact of gravity and take an elevator down a building instead of jumping out a third-story window.

Trusting someone with your heart—and believing that they will not break it—is a huge step of faith. This is what makes loving someone the most powerful expression of faith.

> **From the beginning, God not only prepared faith for you and me to use, He made us creatures of faith. We exercise faith all day long.**

I realize strong feelings are part of love, but there is more to love than feelings. Love is a faith commitment that you will stand with someone even when you do not feel like it. Reliable love transcends feelings.

Vince finally got it. He realized he had no good reason to end his marriage. So, even though his feelings were screaming *Stop!* he decided, by faith in God's Word, to fulfill his role as the unselfish servant leader of his home. Vanessa flew to New Jersey for a week's visit. They set times for work, for Bible study and prayer, for workout sessions, and for good old-fashioned communication. In the end, they made a commitment to honor God in how they would conduct every aspect of their marriage, trusting He would keep them together.

By faith Vince decided to honor his wife—to love her as he loves himself and to lay his life down for her, just as the Bible says to do.

Without faith we would not be able to pray, to have a relationship with God, or to love Him. Thank God He prepared faith as a tool to reach into the unknown.

At some point in each one of our lives, we will be faced with a hopeless situation—at least hopeless in the eyes of those who have not had experience with Jesus. Hope is never dead when faith in God is available to us.

On March 16, 2009, just two months after the divorce papers got mysteriously lost in the mail, Vince and Vanessa renewed their vows at the Rock in San Diego. They're now living in New Jersey. While they both acknowledge that it is going to be a process, their marriage has truly been resurrected by placing their faith in God's promises.

The only way you will do greater things than Jesus did is if you exercise faith in the faithful promises of God and His Word.

ACTIVITIES

Notice how often you do something based on your mood versus acting by faith, trusting that it is the right thing to do.

Dear Lord, I know that it is impossible to please You without faith (Heb. 11:6). Please reveal to me two things pertaining to faith as I read this book. Help me understand how much faith all of the people in this book exercised in their lives through the things that they did. Also, challenge me to live by faith by immediately following through on everything You direct me to do because of what I read.

HEROES

Meet Vince and Vanessa at www.milesmcpherson. com and decide for yourself if the feeling is back.

7

Two Hippies

The Truth

In the beginning was the Word . . .
—John 1:1

These guys must be Charles Manson's cousins.

The TSS store where my girlfriend, Pat, worked was one of those el-cheapo, wannabe department stores where the entire place smelled like Clorox and nothing costs over $50, even the furniture. Well, kinda.

Overhead they announced, "Fifteen minutes. Fifteen minutes until closing." The last few shoppers brushed past me, except for two white dudes I caught sight of. And they were walking toward me.

I watched Pat cashing out. Her thick, jet-black American Indian hair hung to the middle of her back. Her 105-pound figure screamed *America's Next Top Model,* and she never left the house without an hour of makeup prep. I hated waiting for her, but she always looked good.

Me, I was 5 foot 11, 170 pounds, dressed in polyester bell bottoms and a *Saturday Night Fever* shirt. My ten-gallon afro stuck out about half a foot. I looked like a human Blow Pop.

Through the dark store windows I could see my "boyz" on the sidewalk smoking weed. Me and Pat planned to hang with them a little. Then we'd head to her house, talk to her mom for a while, smoke a joint, have sex, and go to sleep.

But as much fun as we had, as much as a nineteen-year-old football player liked sex, I knew deep down inside that it was wrong.

I didn't spend eight years at Our Lady of Lourdes Catholic School wearing a yellow shirt, tie, grey slacks, and penny loafers without learning something about right and wrong.

Sister Rosalita, Sister Wilford, and Sister Agnes were the big three. You did not mess with the sisters. Sister Rosalita, the principal, wore a huge cross that swung from long rosary beads wrapped around her waist. No one challenged Sister Wilford, who was what you might call a big-boned woman. She was the enforcer. Sister Agnes could be sweet, but behind that smile was some major strength. For all their toughness, though, these women loved the Lord, and they loved us too. I learned the fear of God in that school. And most importantly, I got exposed to the Bible.

But five years had gone by since I left Our Lady of Lourdes—four years of public high school, and a year at the University of New Haven. It had also been five years since I'd darkened the door of a church.

C'mon, Pat. I was getting impatient waiting for her to cash out. Then I saw the two guys again. Their holey jeans dragged on the floor. Their oversized, beat-up plaid shirts, light brown hair down to their shoulders, and Jesus beards to the middle of their chests. They looked like leftovers from Woodstock.

What were they doing here? White hippies in this predominantly black neighborhood? *Huh-uh.*

Are they walking toward me? Uh-oh. Those are Bibles in their hands—

I'd smoked a joint before coming in, and I wasn't moving very fast. I just stared at them. Next thing I knew, we were talking.

Woodstock Number One was on my left with his palm-sized Bible open. Woodstock Number Two crowded me on my right.

Where are my boyz when I need them? Those chumps are probably looking through the front door making fun of me.

"Have you been born again?" asked Woodstock Number Two. Even though I was high, something in his voice got me. I wanted to write them off as Jesus freaks, grab Pat, and go home. But something held me on that one spot. I stared down, and all I saw was a Bible.

In the past, when I'd heard the term *born again*, I pictured dudes just like them, looking like Jesus and dancing around with flowers in their mouths. I could feel the last few customers walking by, but I could not look up.

"Would you like to have a relationship with God?" Woodstock Number One asked.

The hippies kept talking. Every time they made a point, they made it from the Bible.

When they told me that I needed to be forgiven, they showed me 1 John 1:8–9.

When they told me that God loved me, they pointed to John 3:16.

When they told me what Jesus had done for me, it was in the Bible, right there in Romans 5:8, staring me in the face.

The Word was the basis of their truth.

It was a truth I could not fight.

I was scared to admit it, but I knew it was true.

•••

"If *You are the Son of God, command that these stones become bread . . .*"

The dry desert wind swirled around Jesus as He lay curled up in the shade of a towering boulder. Sand stuck to His cracked lips. After forty days of fasting, bread would have tasted so good right then.

But He knew where the deep, raspy whisper that seeped from a dark crack in the boulder really came from, and there was something more important to Him than food: obeying the Word of God.

I picture Him turning toward Satan's voice and saying, "It is written, 'Man shall not live by bread alone, but by every word that proceeds from the mouth of God'" (Matt. 4:4).

Suddenly He was swept onto the pinnacle of the Temple, some three hundred feet above Jerusalem.

Again the devil taunted Him: "If *You are the Son of God, throw Yourself down . . .*"—since angels would catch the *real* Messiah (Matt. 4:5–6; Ps. 91:11–12).

58

Jesus did not take the dare. In what must have been a ferocious wind above all of Jerusalem, Jesus rebuffed the devil again. "It is written again, 'You shall not tempt the LORD your God'" (Matt. 4:7; Deut. 6:16).

Lastly, Jesus found Himself even higher, on the top of a high mountain looking at a vision of all the kingdoms of the world.

"All this I will give you," the tempter said, "if you will bow down and worship me."

For the third and last time, Jesus quoted the Bible, saying, "Away with you, Satan! For it is written, 'You shall worship the LORD your God, and Him only you shall serve'" (Matt. 4:10; Deut. 6:13).

Every time Satan tempted Jesus, Jesus responded with the Word of God. He referred to the Scriptures to validate His identity, His mission, His death, and His resurrection (Jonah 1:17; Num. 21:8–10). His arguments with the hypocritical religious leaders of the day were based on biblical truth, because the Scriptures were the authority the Jewish people relied on as the very words of God. The Scriptures were even the basis for the very words He cried out while on the cross (Ps. 22:1).

> **Just as Jesus was *prepared* with the Word already in place as an authoritative truth, so you and I are prepared with God's living Word.**

Can you imagine if the Scriptures had not been established and trusted by the Jewish people? What would Jesus have used to validate His claims? What objective truth would He point the people to? What could He use to verify His claims about His identity and mission?

Just as Jesus was *prepared* with the Word already in place as an authoritative truth, so you and I are prepared with God's living Word.

God has prepared you to do something with the most powerful truth there is, the eternal truth of His own Word.

The Bible.

• •

The hippies clearly had a handle on God's Word.

I kept staring down at their open Bibles. It was as if the pages stared back, daring me to challenge them. I couldn't. I had known, since I was a little kid, that the Bible was God's Word. There was no way I was going to disrespect it. It was more than a book to me. Looking back on that day, it was as if at that very moment God was saying, *I told you I would be here for you when you were ready.*

Pat closed up the register only about ten yards behind me, but she seemed miles away. The store was just about empty now, just me and the hippies.

Well, that's not quite right. Someone else was in that conversation. I felt His presence hanging all over me like a big coat on a cold day. I had the sense that a friend was trying to reach out to me, hoping I would allow Him back into my life. I knew that God was aware of everything I had done wrong. He wasn't mad, though. He missed me.

He wanted me to love Him back.

I felt something like an invisible warm hand on my chest, pressing "urgency" into my heart. I knew my smoking, cursing, and sleeping with Pat did not make God happy.

Another hand grabbed my stomach, causing nervous knots. Think about it—here I was standing in the middle of a department store facing off with two white guys who looked like they lived under a bridge. My boyz were close by, probably laughing at me. And my girlfriend was watching us, wondering what in the world we were talking about.

I didn't know what would happen if I did what these guys were asking me to do.

Was I being challenged to walk away from everything in my life?

It felt as though God was looking straight into my eyes and He knew everything about me. His invisible face was breathing on me, soothing and comforting in love, but at the same time affirming everything the hippies read to me from the worn, note-filled pages of their torn leather Bible.

"Five minutes. Five minutes until closing," the store manager announced through the loudspeaker.

That made it 9:25 p.m. That was the moment I knew I needed God. I needed a relationship with Him the way the hippies described. I bowed my head and by faith asked Jesus to forgive my sins and come live in my heart. I surrendered my life to God.

I felt light-headed. The room began to spin. Something washed off me. My eyes blinked full of tears. I stared at the ground, speechless. I was a different person. I had just spoken to God. No, God had spoken to me.

After the hippies left, Pat walked over. "What was all that about?" I didn't know what to say to her. It was way over my head. I wasn't even sure what it all meant.

But this I know: If the Bible is reliable enough for Jesus to use when being confronted by the devil, how much more should we trust it on a daily basis?

ACTIVITIES

Commit to memorizing a verse by repeating it to yourself several times today. Pick one yourself, or choose from these: "Your word is a lamp to my feet and a light to my path" (Ps. 119:105); "For the word of the LORD is right, and all His work is done in truth" (Ps. 33:4); or "Trust in the LORD with all your heart, and lean not on your own understanding; in all your ways acknowledge Him, and He shall direct your paths" (Prov. 3:5–6).

Dear Lord, I want to learn to apply Your Word to my life. Please give me a hunger and thirst to learn Your Word. I pray that You would bring to my mind a verse that I can use to guide my daily decisions. Thank You, God, for preparing the Word for me.

To find out more about becoming a follower of Jesus, read "Be Something" on page 203.

8

The Invisible Man

Always with You

However, when He, the Spirit of truth, has come, He will guide you
into all truth.

— John 16:13

The white walls were bare, I remember that.

I was daydreaming on the bed in my girlfriend's mother's bedroom.
It was late afternoon in Long Island in 1979. Pat's stepdad was in the
military and gone most of the time. Her mother traveled a lot too.
Whenever I was in town, she let us sleep together in her bed. Kinda
weird, but I got used to it. Hey, I was a nineteen-year-old. I wasn't
going to turn down a king-sized bed with Pat in it.

But now things were different. A week had passed since meeting
the hippies and giving my heart to Jesus. In those seven or so days,
I'd been body-slammed by God. No pot, no sex, no cursing.

I wasn't completely clean, don't get me wrong. We still slept together, but sleep was all we did. For a short while, anyway.

I could hear clinking in the kitchen as Pat washed dishes. She probably would be coming in here soon. As I lay under the blanket on the

edge of the bed, I thought, *What am I going to tell her? Would she even understand the guilty feeling I have?* On the other hand, was I really ready to give this up? We'd been in this routine for almost a year, and to be honest with you, our sin was fun.

But now I not only was aware of my sin—I was feeling bad about it. Ever since that prayer with the hippies. I had admitted being a sinner, and I had asked God to help me change.

What am I doing here? The question bounced around my head in the dim light. My heart burned with an expectation of something more. *I know God wants me to do something for Him with my life. What?*

Then the room began to get brighter.

Now, this is going to sound weird, but against the wall next to the door, I saw grainy dots of oranges, browns, beiges flickering into a shape.

I couldn't move my eyes from that wall. I couldn't move anything. Even my breathing was on hold. I was trippin', big time. The whole thing didn't seem real to me. Well, it was really happening, but it did not look like anything I had ever seen. It was beyond my concept of real.

Within seconds the figure of a man with long hair formed, standing against the wall. I made out a robe hanging to the floor but couldn't see a face. But it was definitely a person. He did not make a sound, and the only thing I could hear was my heart beating.

＊＊＊

Water poured off Jesus' hair, beard, and robe as John the Baptist pulled Him out of the sparkling Jordan River.

The cloudy sky suddenly became clear, and the Holy Spirit, like a dove, gently floated down onto Jesus. The others who had come to the river to be baptized by John had to shield their eyes with their hands. As they looked up, a voice like thunder said, "This is my Son, whom I love; with him I am well pleased" (Matt. 3:16–17 NIV).

Soon after, the Holy Spirit led Jesus into the desert to be tempted by the devil.

From the very beginning of Jesus' ministry, the Holy Spirit was there. Jesus did miracles through the Holy Spirit, He taught with the power of the Holy Spirit, and He was raised from the dead by the Holy Spirit.

The Spirit's partnership in Jesus' life was not limited to His time on earth. The Spirit, who was involved in creation—hovering over the earth, even before there was light—was also involved in preparing Jesus' ministry before He was born.

He revealed to Simeon that Jesus would come. He spoke through Zechariah, John the Baptist's father, announcing Jesus' coming and the purpose for which Jesus would come (Luke 1:67–79). Jesus was conceived by the Holy Spirit. John the Baptist, the one sent to prepare the way for Jesus, declared that Jesus would baptize by the Spirit. These expectations were established by the Holy Spirit Himself through the prophets, long before Jesus began His earthly ministry.

Everything Jesus did, He did in the power of the Holy Spirit.

....

Again, this is going to sound strange, but I really believe this person standing in front of me was God.

I couldn't see His face, but I was sure it was Jesus. I opened my mouth and tried to speak. Nothing came out. I have no idea what I would have said anyway. I tried to lift my arms, but they felt paralyzed.

Was He here to remind me of the commitment I made with the hippies? Even though I was scared, I wanted Him to tell me what was going on—what He wanted me to do. *Say something, Lord!*

It seemed like an hour but was probably only a couple of minutes. I thought of trying to run out of the room, but where the heck was I going to go? I was afraid, but at the same time I felt safe.

He stood next to the bedroom door. He did not move or say a word.

Then He disappeared, slowly and completely.

I couldn't stop looking at the spot on the wall where He had stood. I couldn't believe what I had just seen. Jesus appeared to me. Me! *Wait, why me?* Who was I that He would come to me—and to make it worse, I was lying in my girlfriend's mother's bed!

It took a few minutes for my body to loosen up and be able to move again. I rolled off the bed and walked like a zombie into the kitchen. Pat was still at the sink. She looked at me. I looked at her. Without saying a word, I turned and walked back into the bedroom. *She'd never believe me.*

Reentering the bedroom I thought, *Will He ever come back?*

But since then, I've realized the Invisible Man never left.

When I got in the car with my friends the next day, I knew He was sitting in the backseat with me. When I returned to college, I knew He was in my apartment, in the locker room, and even on the field with me.

Ever since that crazy meeting with the hippies, the Holy Spirit has walked with me. He has been with me ever since birth, but now He lives inside of me. He has been going ahead of me, preparing opportunities for me to do something.

> **After all, before you were born, God prepared you by giving you the Holy Spirit to help you.**

He has been reminding me of the truths of God's Word, encouraging me to trust in it. The Invisible Man knows the deep things of God that pertain to my life (1 Cor. 2:10–12). If my life is going to count, I need to follow His lead, by faith.

Unfortunately He has had to be very patient with me. I have ignored Him so many times. I have wasted so many opportunities.

Are you ignoring Him? Are you taking advantage of the opportunities He provides for you every day? After all, before you were born, God prepared you by giving you the Holy Spirit to help you.

Since that day in the bedroom, I have often found myself staring at walls. In my own bedroom, or in hotel rooms, I have wanted so bad for Him to reappear. But even though He has never revealed Himself to me like He did that day, I see Him all the time in the things He does. We talk, we laugh, we do things together.

He is always with me.

And He is with you too.

ACTIVITIES

Throughout the next twenty-four hours, by faith address the Holy Spirit, the Invisible Man, directly as a Person standing right next to you. Remember,

Jesus refers to the Holy Spirit as *the Helper, the Comforter*. Discuss your concerns and needs with Him, and show Him appreciation as you would a good friend who is acting as your strongest advocate in every area of your life.

Dear Holy Spirit, I know that You are invisible to my natural eye, but my heart acknowledges Your presence in my life, even right now as I read this prayer. I want to have a strong relationship with You. Please open the eyes of my heart that I may see Your hand working in my life.

Watch a clip of the sermon series "The Invisible Man" at www.miles mcpherson.com.

9

Michele

Without a Prayer?

I do not pray for these alone, but also for those who will believe in Me through their word; that they all may be one, as You, Father, are in Me, and I in You; that they also may be one in Us, that the world may believe that You sent Me.

—John 17:20–21

Sarah curled into a fetal position behind the couch.

"Where are you, stupid?" Sarah's mother screamed. "I better not find you hiding from me, or it will be worse."

A tear fell from Sarah's black eye, but she didn't dare move to brush it away.

Good thing the eleven-year-old couldn't hear the mean words. Sarah was deaf. No one in the home knew sign language. Her mother communicated with violence.

Across town, six-year-old Denisse lay on her foster-home bed. She wasn't deaf, but she was hard of hearing. Her foster family knew no sign language either and had a difficult time communicating with her. She ached for Stephanie, her big sister, who lived in yet a different foster home. Stephanie, an eight-year-old, had healthy hearing but suffered from spina bifida, a birth defect of the spinal cord. She often had to be hospitalized for infection.

All three girls felt cut off from the world. They were lonely. Without someone in their life with whom they could communicate, building any positive relationships was very difficult.

That's when God sent Michele.

••

Huffing and puffing, Peter, James, and John jabbed their walking sticks into the rocky path as they followed Jesus up the mountain to pray. At the top, Jesus lifted His hands and face toward the stars and cried out to God. Peter, James, and John, meanwhile, dropped to the ground and fell asleep (Luke 9:32).

Jesus' prayer meeting would rock their world.

While the disciples snored, Jesus' body started glowing, and His clothes began to shine like a hundred fluorescent lights—"shining, exceedingly white, like snow, such as no launderer on earth can whiten them" (Mark 9:3). Then, as though someone turned on two more lightbulbs, Moses and Elijah appeared (Mark 9:4) and began talking to Him.

Peter, James, and John woke up to the glorious scene, and their eyes and mouths popped wide open. Peter asked if the disciples should build a tabernacle for the heavenly visitors, but then a cloud hovered over them. From it they heard a voice say, "This is My Son, My Chosen One; listen to Him!" (Luke 9:35 NASB). They fell on their faces in fear.

As the cloud dissolved, the disciples searched for Moses and Elijah but all they found was Jesus, who stood alone, smiling at them.

Peter, James, and John must have looked at each other, maybe scratching their heads in confusion. They must have been thinking, *What in the world just happened?*

The disciples got a sneak peek—like a photograph developing in front of them—of the results of perfect oneness with God, a condition still in their future. Moses and Elijah, long dead but certainly in heaven, appeared in some glorified and future condition.

Readers of this passage often overlook the fact that the Transfiguration was a direct result of Jesus' prayer.

Jesus prayed all throughout His ministry. He spent forty days and nights in fasting and prayer just before He resisted the temptations of Satan in the wilderness (Matt. 4:1–11). Before He chose His twelve disciples, "He went out to the mountain to pray, and continued all night in prayer to God" (Luke 6:12). He prayed before He fed the five thousand (Matt. 14:15–21). He prayed before He resurrected Lazarus (John 11:41). Before He decided to go to small towns to preach and cast out demons, the Bible says that "a long while before daylight, He went out and departed to a solitary place; and there He prayed" (Mark 1:35). And the list goes on.

Prayer is a gift from God that Jesus did not take for granted. But we must keep in mind that prayer is not simply talking to God; it is a life-transforming form of communication given to us by God. Without prayer, we have no relationship with God. Without relationship, we have no power to bring about a transfiguration in our lives or in the world.

More than 22.5 million Americans have some degree of hearing loss. In fact, one out of every six children has diminished hearing, according to the National Center for Health Statistics.[3]

....

Michele's heart went out to the little girl with big eyes, standing behind the social worker.

"This is Sarah," the woman said. "She just came from the children's shelter. Here's her bag." Sarah had been removed from the abusive home and placed in a protective shelter.

Michele is a thirty-five-year-old, single senior marketing executive for a Fortune 500 company. When a friend's baby son turned out to be deaf, Michele decided to learn American Sign Language. That led to her joining our church's deaf ministry, and eventually filling in for the deaf interpreter.

She was then asked to lead the ministry. Soon she became friends with Lisa, a social worker with the County of San Diego, who founded a ministry at the Rock called Step Up, which places mentors with kids in the foster care system.

The two women talked about how difficult it is to find placements for deaf foster kids. With no licensed foster home for such children in Southern California, deaf children had to be moved to other states, "making reunification with their families really difficult," Michele said.

Prayer is our means of communicating with God.

Without a place to communicate, the closeness that comes from relationship was impossible for the girls. They were constantly covered with a cloud of loneliness, a feeling of isolation. They lacked intimate relationships, and as a result, personal development was hampered.

That's when Michele began praying for ideas on how to help. God answered her.

"God gave me a vision to buy a house and become a foster parent," Michele said matter-of-factly.

Despite a lot of people saying she would be biting off too much, Michele closed on a five-bedroom house in April 2006. Hers is the only licensed deaf foster home in all of Southern California. She has room for up to six children.

The day that Sarah, Michele's first foster child, arrived, Michele knelt and made the sign for hello, a quick salute. "Hello, Sarah," she mouthed. She smiled and pointed to herself. "I'm Michele."

Sarah didn't move.

Few had spoken to her in a language other than violence for a long time. Here was someone speaking to her in love.

Sarah now says, through sign language, that moving into her new home made her feel free for the first time. She was surrounded by people she could communicate with. "It feels like I was born here," she signs.

Stephanie and Denisse joined them in 2007.

Now Stephanie and Denisse don't have to worry when they'll see each other again: they share a bedroom, among a new family that understands them.

The wonder of communication. It's easy to take for granted, but the stories of Sarah, Stephanie, and Denisse remind us what a gift it is.

Imagine if we had no means to communicate with God. What if God was deaf to us, or we were deaf to Him? How could we have a relationship with Him? How could we receive from Him what He wants to communicate with us?

Prayer is our means of communicating with God. Not only do we communicate with God, He also communicates with us, which is the most important part of prayer. The communication we have with God through prayer is not only the transfer of information but access to the actual heart of God. The more we pray with God, the more we become like God.

As you read the prayer at the end of every chapter, trust that God is really listening. Pause for a moment and listen to Him. He may have something good to tell you.

ACTIVITIES

Identify one twelve-minute block of time to spend in daily prayer. Block it out. Get it on your calendar. And then follow through. Using the AWCIPA prayer acronym in the appendix, practice praying every day, two minutes for each letter in the prayer. It will transform your life.

Dear Lord, thank You for the gift of prayer. Thank You for giving us access to a powerful relationship with You through prayer. Even now as I pray to You, please transform my life that I may bring glory to You. Lord, please speak to me as I sit for the next two minutes in silence. I will write down whatever You tell me, God.

HEROES

Meet Michele and her family at www.miles mcpherson.com.

Ph.DO

Learn American Sign Language. To find out more about starting or supporting a ministry to the deaf community, go to www.dosomethingworld.org.

Watch an excerpt from "Bubbles," a sermon series on prayer, at www.milesmcpherson.com.

10

Iva

Long Before You

For we are His workmanship, created in Christ Jesus for good works, which God prepared beforehand that we should walk in them.

— Ephesians 2:10

"Lord, why did You put me in here? Why don't You just let me die?"

No one heard Iva's prayer. The frail ninety-two-year-old woman shifted her weight in her wheelchair and picked up the corner of the handkerchief that she kept safety-pinned to her calico housedress. Wiping her watery blue eyes, she glanced down the hallway of the San Diego nursing facility that had been her home for five years. "What am I doing here?"

White-haired and barely five foot tall, Iva was wrestling with bitterness at being stuck in the long-term care facility for so long.

A hardworking Christian woman all her life, she struggled with how her world had shrunk to a hospital bed and a chest of drawers topped with a few old photos. She shared the room with a stranger, another woman, separated from each other by a thin curtain. Nurses and orderlies came and went. She no longer had her privacy, her independence, or her view of the Oklahoma prairie.

Being in such an institution is often a virtual death sentence. At the least, it's like being in jail. Most people who are admitted never leave. Not all are elderly; some have lingering illnesses. Quite a few are comatose or semi-comatose. Many, the elderly especially, have no visitors. After leading active lives, to be left alone for the last years of your life can be a horribly lonely existence.

Suffering from acute arthritis, Iva was in constant physical pain. But worse than that, her heart hurt. She couldn't help but be resentful at being left there by her family. Iva desperately wanted to return to Oklahoma, but there was no one to take her. Life in the home seemed meaningless.

Just before Christmas, a woman was admitted who appeared to be close to death. "She couldn't talk but made little noises. She couldn't walk or take care of herself," Iva later told Ken, who leads the Rock Church's ministry to convalescent homes.

Iva knew she should pray for the woman, but felt depleted and couldn't make herself seek her out. The next day, rolling down the hallway, Iva bumped into the woman seated in a wheelchair outside of her room. The woman seemed unable to respond to Iva's greetings. "So I laid hands on her and prayed," Iva remembers. "I can't recall the words; I just prayed whatever God laid on my heart."

That's when she realized why she was there.

....

Have you ever wondered why Jesus grew up in Nazareth?

Why wasn't He born a Jew in Brooklyn, Madrid, or Paris? Instead of Bethlehem in the days of Herod, why didn't He come in the time of Napoleon, or FDR, or Barack Obama?

The answer is simple: everything had been prepared for His coming at that time, in that place. Galatians 4:4–5 says, "But when the fullness of the time had come, God sent forth His Son, born of a woman, born under the law, to redeem those who were under the law, that we might receive the adoption as sons."

We know that Jesus, at a young age, had a keen awareness of His mission and the skills to communicate truth. The Hebrew Scriptures and traditions gave Him the moral foundation and parameters within which to accomplish God's purposes for His life. And remember, the Holy Spirit was His ministry partner, not only from the beginning of the ministry on earth, but from before the beginning of time. All of Jesus' preparations would only reach their potential if used in the right environment. God prepared the first-century Middle East as the time and place for Jesus to fulfill His mission.

The Messiah, according to the Scriptures, had to be born in Bethlehem and be a Son of David. He came at a time when the common people felt disenfranchised from the religious elite. The Old Testament law and religious festival calendar were designed as metaphors for the spiritual lessons Jesus would teach. The established blood sacrificial system of Judaism would provide the manner in which He would pay for the sins of the world.

HELP Wanted

Almost 60 percent of people age seventy and older experience some type of loneliness, according to a study by a University of Michigan doctoral student.[4]

Ministry partners were in place when Jesus arrived. John the Baptist began his preaching ministry in preparation before Christ's identity was revealed. Simeon and Anna, local prophets in the temple, had spent years praying in anticipation of a Messiah (Luke 2:25, 36). His disciples were prepared for Him and received Him with readiness and expectancy as they left everything to follow Him.

The Greek language provided a worldwide mode of communication for His message. The road system of the Roman empire made it possible for His disciples to take His message throughout the known world. All of the factors of a God-ordained environment were in place to launch and fulfill what He was sent to do.

It was no coincidence. It was planned. It was necessary. The world was—and is—full of broken sinners in need of a Savior to provide a sinless blood sacrifice, which was why He came.

....

A week or so after Iva laid hands on the sick woman and prayed for her, the woman walked up to her. She was no longer in a wheelchair, no longer speechless nor helpless. Instead of being deathly ill, she was walking—and not only down the hall but out the front door. She was on her way home with her husband. "Thank you for praying for me!" she said to Iva, and hugged her.

For five years Iva had asked God why He had placed her in this gloomy and hopeless situation. Now she began to realize the answer.

God had prepared her to pray. "All my life, I've prayed," she told Ken. "Prayer was my life. I *lived* to pray."

Now, here she was, still alive, surrounded by people with desperate needs.

God has prepared ideal circumstances for you to fulfill what He has called you to do.

These days Ken reports that Iva wheels herself throughout her convalescent home to visit and pray for those patients who are so sick they can barely respond or cannot respond at all to her.

God has prepared ideal circumstances for you to fulfill what He has called you to do.

Sometimes we do not realize how extensive and strategic God's activities have been in our lives until we look back. If you look carefully enough, you will recognize His hand in your circumstances.

You will see His hand on the people He placed in your life, the opportunities He provided for you. You might notice a common characteristic in the kinds of things you have been successful in and those that have consistently been difficult for you. You are who you are and where you are for a reason.

Ephesians 2:10 says, "For we are His workmanship, created in Christ Jesus for good works, which God prepared beforehand that we should walk in them."

God wants you to know that He has gone to great lengths to prepare not only you but the world in which you live, for you to do something.

What you are experiencing today is designed to help you do something. Take advantage of it!

ACTIVITIES

Looking back on your life, make a list of the successes that seemed to come easy for you, circumstances that were designed just for you. Try to identify what was common about them. This will provide insight into the things God has planned for your future.

> *Dear Lord, I know that You have made all of the necessary preparations for me to do something significant with my life. I'm not walking this journey alone. I ask that You open my eyes to see the doors of opportunity that lie before me as well as give me the faith to walk through them. And Lord, give me the discipline to walk away from those opportunities to do something that look important but are really not necessary for me. Please keep me focused on fulfilling Your plan for my life.*

HEROES

Meet Ken at www.milesmcpherson.com.

Ph.DO

Learn to start a ministry in a convalescent home at www.dosomethingworld.org.

DO Something! Myth 2

I must make an instant impact.

The Lies Behind It

- Change always comes immediately.
- We are the ones making the change—not God.
- God's timing is irrelevant.
- You know God is using you when things happen right away.

The Truth

- It's not up to us to bring about change. We only need to obey.
- God makes the changes happen in His time for His purpose.

Scripture

I planted, Apollos watered, but God gave the increase. So then neither he who plants is anything, nor he who waters, but God who gives the increase.

—1 Corinthians 3:6–7

Something to Remember

You are not working for the results. You are working out of obedience.

God will make things happen in His time.

Part 3

Purpose

Obedience

God has given all of us one very simple **purpose**—love, which is summed up in one word: obedience. We prove we love God by obeying God. If we obey God we will do everything He has prepared us to do—nothing more, nothing less.

> For this is the love of God, that we keep His commandments. And His commandments are not burdensome.
>
> —1 John 5:3

11

DeShawn

The Transplant

Then I will give them one heart, and I will put a new spirit within them, and take the stony heart out of their flesh, and give them a heart of flesh, that they may walk in My statutes and keep My judgments and do them; and they shall be My people, and I will be their God.

—Ezekiel 11:19–20

DeShawn's biological mother abandoned him when he was ten. When Mike became his mentor through a local agency, DeShawn was a shy, skinny twelve-year-old living with thirty kids in a group home.

Mike visited DeShawn every week. They played laser tag, threw the football around, went to ball games, or just hung out watching movies. DeShawn attended the Rock Church with Mike and his wife, Renee; he even joined them in the hospitality ministry. They greeted visitors and took the church offering.

But in a little over a year, when he would turn thirteen, DeShawn was going to "age out" of his current group home. That meant being uprooted and starting new relationships and routines in a new home. That's when God began challenging Mike to take his relationship with DeShawn to another level and become his foster parent.

There was one problem, though. Renee wanted no part of full-time motherhood.

When Mike and Renee married, they agreed they did not want kids. Renee had become comfortable with having Mike all to herself. She liked their lifestyle. Yes, Mike had become a mentor to a twelve-year-old, and Renee enjoyed getting to know DeShawn. But he always returned to the group home, and Renee and Mike had their home to themselves. That's how they liked it.

But God, the Great Physician, was about to do heart surgery.

....

Running behind the crowd in an attempt to see Jesus, a short tax collector named Zacchaeus jumped up and down, trying to look over the shoulders of the crowd.

None of the people lining the street would let him through. Zacchaeus was one of the most hated men in town.

Tax collectors were charged with collecting taxes from the Jewish people on behalf of the oppressive Roman government. Their scam was to collect more than people actually owed and pocket the difference. As a chief tax collector who oversaw other tax collectors, Zacchaeus ran a pyramid scheme with several collectors reporting to him.

So it was no surprise that the people were not willing to "help a brother out" so he could see the Lord.

But Zacchaeus did not get to be a chief tax collector by being a dummy. He ran ahead and climbed a tree that he figured Jesus would pass. Sure enough, the Lord walked by. Then Jesus stopped. He looked up and called Zacchaeus down. Not only that, He invited himself to Zacchaeus's house.

The people got upset. This Zacchaeus guy was one of the greediest in Jericho. He took advantage of everyone in town for personal gain. Certainly Jesus could have visited more reputable people. Why would Jesus go to *his* house?

Luke 19:7 says, "But when they saw it, they all complained, saying, 'He has gone to be a guest with a man who is a sinner.'"

Zacchaeus wasn't concerned with accusations of being a sinner; he just knew that at that moment he was "the man." Perhaps with his arm around his new best friend all the way home, Zacchaeus did not know what God, the Great Physician, was about to do.

DeShawn continued to visit Mike and Renee's house, but at the end of the day, he would return to the group home—and that's how Renee liked it.

Then one day, sitting on her stylish tan leather couch in front of her 47-inch big screen, Renee heard God speak to her. *You should bring this child into your home and become a foster parent.*

She shook her head.

This can't be right, she thought. *This cannot be right. I do not want kids.*

Her heart was simply not into being a parent. She listed all the excuses she could think of. *I have no experience at being a parent. I wouldn't be able to handle all of the responsibility. I have no local family to support me.*

From July to October Renee never told Mike of the battle she was fighting with God. She kept convincing herself that the still small voice would go away.

Then God nudged her over the edge. *Of course you can't do it, not alone*, she heard Him tell her. *You will need to lean upon Me.*

She finally gave in, and her heart transplant was complete. "Okay, Lord, I can foster someone like DeShawn."

A few nights later, sitting in bed next to her, Mike turned toward Renee. "I need to ask you something—"

Before he could finish, she said, "I already know what it is, and the answer is yes."

God had to replace Renee's selfish heart with an unselfish one for her to express the self-sacrificial love DeShawn needed. Fulfilling our purpose to obey God is not something our sinful hearts naturally want to do, especially to the degree He wants us to do it. Because we are "naughty by nature,"

HELP *Wanted*

More than half a million children in the U.S. reside in some form of foster care, and placements have dramatically increased over the past ten years.[5]

we think of ourselves first. When we do think of helping people, our generosity is tainted with, *Will I enjoy it? How long will it take? What will I get out of it?*

To put it bluntly, that attitude breaks God's heart.

He needs to give us a brand-new heart altogether.

....

As Jesus sat in Zacchaeus's house, His host underwent some divine surgery. Luke 19:8 says, "Zacchaeus stood and said to the Lord, 'Look, Lord, I give half of my goods to the poor; and if I have taken anything from anyone by false accusation, I restore fourfold.'"

Zacchaeus had a change of heart. He not only admitted being guilty of ripping people off but was willing to go way out of his way to make things right.

....

One day soon after moving in, DeShawn came in from the pool after swimming. He was wrapped in a beach towel but unnaturally cold. That night he lay tossing and turning, grunting from pain. The next morning he was bent over with nausea.

Within hours he was diagnosed with cardiomyopathy, a life-threatening condition that prevents hearts from pumping blood properly.

You cannot fulfill your purpose without a heart transplant.

It turns out many cardiomyopathy patients are young, African American males, like DeShawn. Although the condition is often fatal, his doctors thought it could be treated, and they sent him home with a prescription.

Three days later DeShawn was in a Life Flight helicopter to Los Angeles, where he would be hospitalized until a compatible heart was located for a transplant. The doctors told Mike and Renee the wait would be between two and six months. The San Diego couple committed to stay in L.A. as long as it would take to bring DeShawn home healthy.

As soon as DeShawn went to L.A. to wait for his heart, Mike and Renee asked the church for prayer. DeShawn got his new heart, not in the typical six, three, or even two months, but in one week.

The surgery took eight hours, and DeShawn left the hospital seven days later.

The speed at which DeShawn got his heart is amazing. But so is the significance of what God did for Renee. God gave Renee a spiritual heart transplant so that she could be with DeShawn for his physical heart transplant.

Who knows what would have happened if Mike and Renee were not DeShawn's foster parents? The fact is, if Renee had not opened herself to allowing God to invade her sense of privacy, the space of her home, and her lifestyle, DeShawn might not be alive today.

How far are you willing to go to allow Jesus to give you a new heart, one that will obey God at all costs? Who will not get the second chance they need because you have resisted a heart transplant? The Bible tells us to love God with your entire heart, mind, and soul (Matt. 22:37), and we can only do that by surrendering our heart to him so he can give us a new one.

You cannot fulfill your purpose without a heart transplant. The Great Physician wants to remove your heart of stone and give you a heart of flesh, one that will beat at His command (Ezek. 36:26), one that desires to love everyone He sends your way.

ACTIVITIES

Hold a small ice cube in your hand and let it melt. As you do, thank God for continually melting your heart to keep His ways.

Dear Lord, I know that my heart is more selfish than I want to admit. Please give me a new heart, one that wants to fulfill Your desires, not mine (Jer. 17:9; Ps. 51:10).

Ph.DO

Become a foster parent. Find out how at www.dosomethingworld.org.

12

Sista' Bev

New Eyes

For the LORD does not see as man sees; for man looks at the outward appearance, but the LORD looks at the heart.

—1 Samuel 16:7

Beverly felt a dozen eyes burn through her like lasers as she slipped through the narrow visitor entrance at Donovan prison. Heart racing, she kept her eyes down and followed her guide through the yard.

I want to leave this place today, the petite, middle-aged secretary thought. *Please, God, help me get out of here.*

Head down, she ignored her apprehension as the pastor over our church's prison ministry led her across the yard to the tiny cinder-block chapel. She would not look at the men who stood in groups—blacks with blacks, Asians with Asians, whites with whites, browns with browns. Some were jogging, doing push-ups and chin-ups, or playing basketball. Most just wandered around.

What are they thinking? Beverly wondered. *There are murderers out there. Gang members. Drug dealers. Someone is going to shout something, I just know it. What should I do?*

The prison yard at Richard J. Donovan Correctional Facility in San Diego County was the size of a soccer field, enclosed by the bullet-gray, two-story structures that housed the felons. A paved path rimmed the yard. A twenty-foot-high concrete fence enclosed the medium- to high-risk complex. Razor wire, like a wicked Slinky, twisted across the top. Sharpshooters stared down on the inmates from gray towers that overshadowed the corners of the yard.

What am I doing here?

What did she have to say that criminals would want to hear? She'd never been to a prison, knew no "bangers," and had never experienced the poverty or neglect that most of the inmates had. She was just a suburban, middle-class white woman whose husband had walked out on her four years ago; a survivor of breast cancer; a follower of Christ who had been forced to cling to God and trust in Him for everything.

Her stomach was in knots. *How many guys will be there? Will they listen to me? Will they heckle me?*

The chaplain stopped and Beverly looked up. They had come to an unmarked door. It was open. Inside she saw folding chairs set up in rows facing the door. Most of the men, fifty or sixty of them, were already seated. They were dressed in light blue collarless shirts and denim bottoms. Some wore dark beanies. Most had tattoos: on foreheads, necks, chests, arms, hands, ankles.

This is a chapel? Beverly thought. She moved to a corner at the back. She needed a moment to collect herself and pray before speaking. Then a pair of bright green eyes surrounded by brown dreadlocks appeared inches from her face.

David, a former gang member, jammed her up.

"So, lady, what do you have to offer, coming in here? You've never experienced this life. What you got to say?"

Beverly wanted to melt into the floor.

• •

Surrounded by a large crowd, Jesus walked with His disciples into a city called Nain. His reputation was spreading; word that He healed a centurion's sick son made Him a magnet for people in need.

Just as they reached the city gate, they met a second crowd coming out of town. It was a funeral procession for a young man. His

To fulfill our purpose to love the broken world, we need to see the brokenness of the world with the eyes of love.

body was being carried in an open casket down the street.

Jesus spotted the widow, the mother of the dead man. Luke records His reaction this way: "*When the Lord saw her*, He had compassion on her and said to her, 'Do not weep'" (Luke 7:13, emphasis added).

Surrounded by a multitude of mourners and gawkers, Jesus focused on what He saw in one person, a mother grieving her only son.

Jesus looked at the woman's face, but He saw the pain in her heart. He felt her grief and her sense of hopelessness.

Her pain became His own.

···

Beverly gazed at the 220-pound gang member glaring down at her.

She saw the eyes of an angry man who had been walking down a hard road for many years. Her love saw his pain and loneliness. She saw a guy who challenged her prison ministry "credentials" as a way to protect himself from being disappointed once again.

Then she thought of the pain she had experienced, living separate from her husband for four years, after months and years of broken dreams and disappointment. She thought of hearing she had breast cancer, facing the prospect of death while undergoing painful surgery and radiation.

Beverly thought, *I'm not that much different than you. I have experienced hurt and rejection too.* She recognized her painful past in David's drama. She remembered how unworthy and insecure her husband's leaving made her feel. Now she was watching those feelings in David lash out at her.

She swallowed, and smiled up at the only roughneck she had ever met.

"You're right. I've never been in prison, and I'm probably the last person you would ever imagine coming here," she began. A few other guys nearby were listening too. "But I know I'm supposed to be here. I'm supposed to come in here and talk about hope, about how Jesus has changed my broken life and how he can change yours too."

At that moment, Beverly became qualified, but not by what she said as much as what she saw. Looking at David, Beverly's heart saw a guy who needed what God had given her. Hope!

Looking at David, her heart saw a part of herself. She couldn't see David for what he was until she remembered who she was.

Sista' Bev now ministers monthly in "the joint." In fact, inmates have started recruiting others to come to chapel when she's scheduled to speak.

Sista' Bev's heart sees the inmates as God sees them. She offers them hope—hope through the Lord.

Inmates now regularly tell her of their wives wanting a divorce, of not knowing if their wives are cheating on them, of worrying about who is raising their children. They are weighed down by the guilt of the crime that landed them in prison in the first place.

Her feminine insights have helped the inmates appreciate the pain and hurt their wives are going through. Separated from her husband but still married, she tells the inmates that she prays for him daily. Her faithfulness has been an eye-opening lesson to them. Many of them have never heard marriage advice from a woman, much less a godly one.

When you look at people, do you see them as man sees or as God sees? Remember, "man looks at the outward appearance, but the LORD looks at the heart" (1 Sam. 16:7). More importantly, do you see yourself as God sees you? Loved, but still in progress?

Mother Teresa said that the worst poverty of all is loneliness, the absence of love. If your love can see the pain and hopelessness in someone's heart, there is a good chance your love will speak to them; there is a good chance your love will encourage them. Be willing to make a sacrifice for them, giving them hope they do not have.

HELP
Wanted

More than 1 in 100 American adults were incarcerated at the start of 2008.[6]

Walking into the chapel, Sista' Bev's fear was fueled by what she thought was inadequate relevance, experience, and training. But the more Beverly saw the inmates' brokenness, and the more she was able to reveal her heart to them by being transparent about her failed marriage, the more she was able to share about her fear of what her cancer would do to her. The more power her ministry was to them.

To fulfill our purpose to love the broken world, we need to see the brokenness of the world with the eyes of love. We need to be willing to share our own brokenness. We need to allow God's love to show us people's hopelessness as Jesus sees it.

ACTIVITIES

When you greet people today with the typical "How are you doing?" do your best to mean it. Stop and ask a second time, and wait for the truth. Be honest with them about your feelings. Then spend a few seconds encouraging them.

Dear God, please show me the spiritual need of those I come in contact with. Give me a sensitive, loving heart that will see people as You see them and love them according to their real need.

HEROES

Meet Beverly and her fellow prison ministry volunteers at www.milesmcpherson.com.

Ph.DO

Start a prison ministry. To find out more, go to www. dosomethingworld.org.

13

The Cook

Even the Unlovable

But God demonstrates His own love toward us, in that while we were still sinners, Christ died for us.

—Romans 5:8

There wasn't a light on in the house, at least none that could be seen from the street, but that wasn't going to stop us.

Danny told me he had a new contact for cocaine. Just after dark we drove down into the "hood," a rough neighborhood of older one-story homes in southeast San Diego. The bars on the windows were a reminder that bad things happened on that block. A small, still voice whispered, "Be careful, Miles."

Even though I had prayed with the hippies and been visited by the Invisible Man, God Himself, I was not living for God yet.

Danny was one of the most gifted athletes playing for the Chargers that season. He was a 6-foot-2, 190-pound defensive back, a self-proclaimed ladies' man. Smooth cocoa-brown skin, straight pearly white teeth, and a mustache. The brother swore he belonged in *GQ*. Despite his clean-cut look, he and I were on our way to play with the devil.

Danny knocked on the door while I stood at the bottom of the steps, glancing out into the street. Here I was paranoid about who might know we were going into this house, and we hadn't even gotten high yet.

The brother who opened the door looked like he had just woken up. Maybe four inches shorter than Danny, with nappy, uncombed hair, he was rubbing his eyes as he motioned us in. I assumed he was the dealer. We squeezed through the door and stood in the dimly lit living room. The house was quiet except for a little music coming from a back room.

Danny's friend immediately walked down the hall and returned, handing Danny a white matchbox-sized package of folded paper. Danny handed it to me.

The two of them made small talk, and I heard the word *crack*.

Danny had done crack several times before, but not me. I vowed that I would never smoke that stuff.

I had said that about cocaine, though. I had said that about pot too, which by then I had been doing for about six years.

They told me a guy was making crack in the bathroom. I wasn't going to smoke it, but being a curious person, I asked to see how it was made. The dealer led me to the back of the house, knocked on the bathroom door, and opened it. I had no idea what I expected to see.

There, on a stool next to the toilet, sat a skeleton covered with dark brown skin and dressed in shorts and a wife-beater T-shirt. The skeleton was trembling. I watched it dip a small spoon in a jar.

The cook—I don't remember his name—welcomed me into his "kitchen" with a soft "wazzup" and a slight nod. Then he went back to work.

The bathroom smelled like my high school chemistry class. There were no typical amenities. No toothbrushes, toothpaste, soap, towels, or rugs. Instead it had small bowls of liquids and utensils on the sink. A hot plate was plugged into the wall socket and sat on the back of the toilet, along with a small scale used to weigh the powder to make the "rock."

I was careful not to crowd him. I had questions, but I figured I would let him take the lead and initiate conversation when he felt like it. I sat on the edge of the bathtub for about thirty minutes, watching him mix and cook his chemicals.

The process cooked cocaine down to its most potent form, to be placed in a pipe and smoked. The powerful smoke would send users into a euphoria-induced meltdown so strong they would forget you were in the room with them. This I would soon witness firsthand.

I couldn't take my eyes off the cook. His skinny, ashy body actually belonged to a young guy, but one who had been torn up from drug use. The whole time I was there he kept scratching himself.

I didn't know anything about him, but I kept thinking about him and how messed up his life was. It was as if I was feeling sorry for him. But why would I be? He chose this life for himself.

Then it hit me. Maybe Jesus was trying to love him through me.

• •

Jesus loved everyone He came in contact with. Even those considered unlovable and untouchable by the average joe.

In the first chapter of the book of Mark, there is a story of Jesus being approached by a leper. In those days, people the Bible calls lepers were required to cry out "Unclean! Unclean!" everywhere they went so that people could keep at least six feet away. The disease was thought to be very contagious. If the wind was blowing, you needed to be thirty feet away. There was no cure, nowhere to get help.

But this leper, based on what he had heard, believed that Jesus could heal him. When he saw Jesus coming, he walked up to Him, knelt down, and said, "If You are willing, You can make me clean" (Mark 1:40).

Unlike everyone else who passed by the leper, Jesus reached out His hand and touched him. Up to then, no one would ever get within six feet of this guy, and that was on a good weather day.

What was Jesus' motivation? The Bible says Jesus was moved with compassion for the guy. He loved the leper so much that He reached far outside the cultural comfort zone to express that love.

• •

So, I was sitting there on the edge of that bathtub thinking, *Does Jesus love this crack cook too?*

At that moment Jesus seemed to want to express His love to this cook. But this guy, unlike the leper, wasn't seeking Jesus. He was busy making crack. So why was the scene so heavy on my mind and heart? What did his problem have to do with me?

I glanced in the bathroom mirror and found the answer. *What was the difference between me and the cook?* I asked myself. We were in the same place doing practically the same thing. I was beginning to waste away just like him—I just happened to be in good shape from football. Maybe I was the more pitiful one in the room. I had a new heart, but I wasn't using it.

· ·

Jesus' ministry was consumed with loving broken people even when they ignored Him. This cook was the type of guy people avoid. Yet for some reason, here I was, sitting in a bathroom alone with him. And to make things more crazy, I was thinking about how much God loved him.

After all, your purpose is to love the unlovable in the eyes of the world, just as Christ did.

On top of that, ever since I had walked in the house Jesus had been trying to get my attention. But why here, why now? This wasn't church, it was a crack house.

"Miles, I love that guy," a voice kept whispering through my mind. *"Miles, I love you too."*

To be honest, it was distracting me.

Here I was, a pro athlete in a crack house. Jesus had blessed me with talent and a great opportunity. But I was throwing it away.

In a similar way, this cook, I am sure, had seen better days, and that was breaking Jesus' heart. And for some reason, it was getting to me too. Maybe because it was breaking Jesus' heart.

· ·

Maybe there are people in your life wasting away right before your eyes. They might not be a scrawny druggie, cooking crack, but their life is definitely going in the wrong direction. For some reason, God has placed you in their life. Maybe He has shown you something in them that they cannot see. Maybe He has shown you something in them that He wants you to pray for.

Take a risk and reach out to them. Maybe you need to be willing to sacrifice your time and energy for them. After all, your purpose is to love the unlovable in the eyes of the world, just as Christ did. (And keep in mind, you might be the unlovable one.)

ACTIVITIES

Identify the "cook" in your life: someone headed in the wrong direction. In your own way, express to them that God has not forgotten about them, that He loves them. Write them a note, send them an email, or pay them a visit.

Maybe that "cook" is you.

Dear Lord, I know that my purpose is to love those You bring into my life. Please remind me that it includes those who may be strangers to me, those who could benefit from a kind word from You through me. Give me the courage to express Your love toward them.

HEROES

Meet a former crack cook at www.milesmcpherson. com.

14

Carter

"I Love Him"

Assuredly, I say to you, inasmuch as you did it to one of the least of
these My brethren, you did it to Me.

—Matthew 25:40

"Pastor Bobby!"

Robert Yates was leading a dozen adults from a van into a service
at the Rock Church. Most were walking hand in hand. Not all their
pants reached their ankles; not all their shirts covered their stomachs.
A few wore thick glasses.

"Somebody just had an accident, Pastor Bobby!"

Yates, a smiling middle-aged man whose beard and frame makes
him look like a youngish Santa Claus, was a little new at this ministry to people with physical or developmental needs. He was already stressed at making sure he didn't lose anyone. *What now?* he
thought.

Known as Pastor Bobby, Yates felt God had called him to start the
Luv-Em-Up ministry to the disabled. He loved serving people. And
as a former social worker who had run drug and alcohol diversion
programs in prisons, he had seen a lot.

But he was also the type of guy who gagged at baby diapers.

"What happened?" Pastor Bobby said, dreading the answer.

His worst nightmare was standing at the back of the crowd, his pant legs soiled and dripping onto the sidewalk. Tommy, a developmentally disabled man in his forties who was usually laughing, looked shocked and humiliated. "I'm sorry, Pastor Bobby. I pooped my pants."

Bobby's stomach flipped. *Oh no. What do I do now?*

"Everybody! Follow me!" he barked, and frantically started searching for a restroom. The men and women of Luv-Em-Up followed quietly and waited on benches outside as Bobby led Tommy into a nearby men's room, trying not to throw up.

"Here, Pastor Bobby. Let me do that for you."

Bobby looked up and saw Carter, another Luv-Em-Up member, start to take off his jacket and roll up his sleeves. Carter was in his mid-fifties with gray hair. Like Tommy he was developmentally disabled. But Carter was pretty good at communicating. He was always the first to welcome newcomers with a big smile and sit with them.

Bobby stood staring at Carter for a moment, nausea rising in his throat.

"Pastor Bobby, you have to move so that I can take care of Tommy," Carter said.

"Are you sure, Carter?"

Carter looked at Tommy and smiled. Bobby couldn't believe what he heard next.

"It would be my pleasure. I love him."

· ·

Like little kids asking their father to tell them a bedtime story, Jesus' disciples pleaded with Him to tell them about the kingdom of God. He told them a story about His second coming.

With the brightness of a thousand lightning bolts and the roar of ten thousand cracks of thunder, the Son of Man will appear with His angels to judge the world. He will sit on His throne, and I envision angels as far as sight can see hovering above Him with their motionless wings extended, singing *Holy, Holy, Holy*. I picture light brighter than the sun blasting out of the scars on His hands and feet and filling the heavens. Even though millions will be judged, all will feel intimately close to Him.

In the blink of an eye, the singing of millions of souls will rise from the right side of his throne, a position of favor with God. In that same instant, the cries and groans of tens of millions will rise from the left side, the position of God's displeasure (Matt. 25:31–46).

Like two waves crashing, the rejoicing and the wailing will meet at the throne, and the Son of Man will judge right and wrong. He will stand in front of His throne, and I imagine the angels' wings contracting as they bow in silence.

The Son of Man will look to those on the right and say to them, "Well done, good and faithful servants. You loved me, 'for I was hungry and you gave Me food; I was thirsty and you gave Me drink; I was a stranger and you took Me in; I was naked and you clothed Me; I was sick and you visited Me; I was in prison and you came to Me'" (see Matt. 25:23, 35–36).

Then to the left He will turn and say, "Depart from Me, you cursed, into the everlasting fire prepared for the devil and his angels: for I was hungry and you gave Me no food; I was thirsty and you gave Me no drink; I was a stranger and you did not take Me in, naked and you did not clothe Me, sick and in prison and you did not visit Me" (Matt. 25:41–43).

When He sits down, the screams of confused souls will vibrate from both sides of the throne. "When did we see You sick or in prison, naked, or hungry? When did You ever need ministering to?" (see Matt. 25:37–39).

Then the Son of Man will say, "Assuredly, I say to you, inasmuch as you did it to one of the least of these My brethren, you did it to Me" (Matt. 25:40).

Fulfilling your purpose to love the world includes ministering to *the least of these*, those who cannot pay you back. Loving *the least of these* is not only about what you can give them but what Jesus Himself will teach you about love *through* them.

....

As he drove home that night, Bobby had to pull over to the side of the road in tears.

Why can't I love like that?

He thought about the men and women of Luv-Em-Up.

They hug and tell him they love him every hour. They never seem to see anything negative in Bobby. If he trips, they laugh and say, "Do it again!" They accept him for who he is, for how he is. No questions asked.

His time with them is his most unguarded time of the week. Even though he is called to encourage them, they are the ones who teach him.

Parked on the side of the road, he thought through all that had happened that day.

After leaving Carter with Tommy, he had run to the van in a panic to try to find something Tommy could change into. All he found was a small towel. Jogging back, he had seen Carter coming out of the restroom, the front of his shirt and pants soaking wet. In one hand he held Tommy's hand; in the other he held a bundle of Tommy's messy clothes. Tommy was clean and dry now—and wearing only Carter's jacket tied around his waist.

"Okay. Let's go," Carter had said simply, heading toward the church sanctuary.

Bobby stood there in amazement. Carter was acting like nothing happened, as if he had done nothing extraordinary. "Hold on, Carter. We can't go in now. We'll have to go home, but we'll have fun there too. Thank you for helping Tommy."

"Don't thank me, Pastor Bobby. He is my friend. I love him," he said again.

When the group returned to their board-and-care home, Bobby was helping Tommy out of the van. "Pastor Bobby?" he said with sad eyes. "Carter prayed for me in the bathroom when he cleaned me up. He loves me, huh?"

Bobby was blown away.

"My life changed that day," he would later say. "My level of love and service was brought to a new level. I still, to this day, seek that kind of unconditional love."

HELP *Wanted*

Nine million, or 13 percent of, children in the United States have a special health-care need.[7]

How many times have you seen a group of Carters and Tommys walking down the street, and felt sorry for them—not realizing that they could teach you a lesson or two about how to love people? How many times have you looked down at the poor, not realizing God may have chosen them to be rich in faith, or the weak, not realizing they may have a level of inner strength you'll never have.

Your purpose of expressing God's love will lead to receiving a lesson about God's love.

Loving the "least of these"—people who cannot pay you back, or increase your social status—is not an annual charity event. It is not something to do to feel good. It is not how you get into heaven, but it is evident in the lives of those who are going there.

Your purpose of expressing God's love will lead to receiving a lesson about God's love. Jesus plainly said that ministering to the least of these was equivalent to ministering to Him.

Why?

When we are weak, we become strong in God's strength, because it is during those weak times in our lives that His strength is expressed in the purest form (2 Cor. 12:10). It is that pure expression of God's love that we encounter when we minister to the least of these, and when we do, we get a big lesson in love.

Jesus taught His disciples that there are specific common denominators of those who believe in Him. One of those characteristics is their past history of expressing love to people in need: the least of these. Our ministry to them is an indicator of how well we are fulfilling our purpose to love people.

DO SOME THING

ACTIVITIES

Where are you right now? Home? Work? An airplane? A waiting room? Wherever you are, try to identify someone either in your immediate surroundings or within a one-mile radius who might be, in the eyes of the world, the "least of these."

Done? Good. Now all you have to do is show them God's love. Go to it.

Dear Lord, please open the eyes of my heart that I may see who You want me to minister to. Please protect me from my pride so that I may receive a lesson from those who appear to be less fortunate.

HEROES

Meet Bobby and Carter at www.milesmcpherson. com.

Ph.DO

To start a disabilities ministry, go to www.do somethingworld.org.

15

Francisco

Multiplication

Go therefore and make disciples of all nations, baptizing them in the name of the Father and of the Son and of the Holy Spirit.

—Matthew 28:19

Francisco shivered as he walked up the cement steps to the next house. The ten-year-old noticed that the curtains behind the wrought-iron window bars were still drawn. Inside the people were probably still asleep. He switched the plastic bag of eggs to his other shoulder and pounded on the door.

"¡*Vete!* We don't want any!" a man's voice shouted through the window.

Francisco sighed and turned away just as the sun was coming up over the hills behind the barrio. He was always glad to see dawn, because then he would begin to warm up. Another half hour before he had to head for school.

Walking the rocky Tijuana streets in winter at 6:30 was hard, but he had to earn his daily quarter for lunch.

His mother made corn tortillas by hand, earning a dollar a day. When she was sick, she and Francisco's four siblings didn't eat anything except what they might have at school.

Francisco remembered a time when he was seven. It was on one of those "Mama sick" days. The neighbor who helped keep an eye on the children had asked him what the family would be eating that day. Barefoot and dirty, Francisco said, "We're not eating today. Mama is sick."

The neighbor asked him to run to the store for her. She'd give him something. When he returned, she was scraping rice and beans on the bottom of a pan. She handed him the pan. That was the meal for his siblings and him.

As he walked out of her house, Francisco had looked up at the sky through tears and had vowed never to let that happen to him again.

The next house had a light on in the window. A pot of geraniums on the front step made the place seem friendlier than some of the shacks Francisco had approached. He knocked.

When the door opened, he froze in embarrassment.

•••

Walking along the seashore, Jesus approached two fishermen who were grabbing the ends of their nets, stretching them out and spreading them over the surface of the lake. As they prepared to cast another net, Jesus interrupted with a simple command: "Follow Me, and I will make you fishers of men" (Matt. 4:19). The Bible says they *immediately left their nets and followed Him.*

He gave a similar command to Levi, who was sitting at his tax office. Jesus said, "Follow me" (Matt. 9:9), and Levi arose and followed Him.

He repeated this process until He had His twelve disciples. They walked with Jesus for three years, learning the intricacies of being fishers of men. The disciples witnessed Him exercise supernatural power through His miracles. They listened to Him teach the spiritual insight of God's Word and watched Him take on hypocritical religious leaders. And He told them that they would do all He had done and more, once He left to go back to the Father in heaven.

Just before He left them for the last time, He reminded them of their mission.

In Matthew 28:19, He said, "Go therefore and make disciples of all the nations, baptizing them in the name of the Father and of the Son and of the Holy Spirit."

Jesus did not come just to love His twelve disciples or those He would personally heal, deliver, or encourage. He came to set in motion a movement that would last far beyond His time on earth.

He strategically established a system that would multiply His efforts through His twelve disciples and reach the world. He did this by investing Himself in them until they were ready to invest themselves in others.

Jesus' discipleship process was not limited to an information transfer process. It was a life transfer process designed to lead His followers in fulfilling the individual purposes of their lives which took unpredictable twists and turns.

....

Francisco's fifth-grade teacher, Señora Vicki, stood in the doorway.

"*Hola*, Francisco," she said, gazing at him with a puzzled look on her face. She was a short, round, middle-aged woman who Francisco sensed was kind. "What are you doing here this morning? Isn't school starting soon?"

His cheeks suddenly warm, Francisco mumbled that he was selling eggs for lunch money. Señora Vicki smiled again and said she would be happy to buy two.

Francisco doesn't remember much after that, except running home as fast as he could.

He had been running the mean, rocky streets of Tijuana all his life.

He couldn't remember much of his first five years. At six, he and his siblings lived in a plywood shack without plumbing or electricity. It was at the end of an alley where people dumped and burned their garbage. His neighbors were prostitutes, drug dealers, and other "have-nots." He and his siblings bathed from a bucket of water once a week. For most of the first ten years of his life, he had lice.

Practically speaking, Francisco was on his own. At that time, his mother worked in San Diego during the week as a maid. Her employers would drive her to visit once a week and give her thirty minutes with the children in the car. That was it. A pair of street vendors looked after him, his three-year-old sister, a one-year-old brother, and an infant brother. To help out, Francisco sold Chiclets gum on the street.

When he was around six and a half, his mother came back to Tijuana and began making tortillas for a living. Still, survival was top priority; school was an afterthought. Having rarely eaten a balanced meal growing up, he was one of the smallest kids in his class.

He missed the first grade and had been behind ever since. Now in fifth grade, his seat at the back of the class was symbolic of his grades. He had no confidence he would ever do well in school. He certainly had no role models. His father had long ago abandoned the family, and his mother hadn't gone past the third grade.

The day after knocking on Señora Vicki's door, Francisco stood up and got ready to file out with his chattering fifth-grade classmates on their way to recess.

"Francisco, would you come here, *por favor*?" Señora asked.

What did she want? Francisco's teachers usually never spoke to him unless he was in trouble. Did he forget to turn in his homework? Would she make fun of him about the eggs?

He prepared himself to get hit, which teachers were allowed to do in those days. He kept his eyes on the floor.

"Francisco," he heard Señora Vicki say, "I would like you to represent the class in the reading contest."

Stunned, Francisco looked up. Señora was smiling.

HELP
Wanted

Of the American families whose parents do not have a high school diploma, more than 7 million, or 84 percent, of the children in these families are considered low income.[8]

"Me?"

"*Sí*. I've been watching you. I think you could do a really good job," she said.

Francisco felt a warmth spread from his head to his toes. He accepted the challenge.

Even though Francisco was convinced he would never get good grades, he desperately wanted to succeed. Without knowing it, Francisco was looking for someone to believe in him. So when Señora Vicki offered him some hope, he grabbed on and never let go.

> **Your job is not to make them like you but to help them become the person God created them to be—so that they may fulfill their purpose of obeying God.**

Francisco studied hard. While he did not win the contest, the experience boosted his confidence. From then on, he never got lower than a B the rest of his life. Even when he moved into sixth grade and beyond, Señora Vicki continued to challenge him. Whether he was on the playground or walking down the hall in school, she would stop and ask how he was doing.

That constant presence was a reminder to Francisco of her belief that he was someone with potential. She was right.

Francisco went on to go to school six days a week while working seven days and every summer. He would later immigrate to the United States, graduate from Ohio State University with a degree in physical education, play professional soccer for five years, and spend twenty years as a business executive with McDonald's Corporation.

Known as Frank, he served as National Director of Training for the entire company; Corporate Vice President of Franchise Relations, Strategy and Innovation for the U.S.; Corporate VP in the Restaurant Solutions Group, which oversees operations around the world; and adviser to the president.

After leaving McDonald's, Frank formed a consulting group to help CEOs in strategy and leadership. He also happens to be my personal accountability partner, and I love him like a brother.

"To this day I don't know why Señora Vicki cared for me, but I'm grateful she did," he told me once.

Jesus called us to make disciples, people who will multiply in others what you invested in them.

Without disciples, Christianity would not have lasted a generation, let alone thousands of years.

If He hasn't already, God is able to send you a "dry sponge of a soul," ready to soak up everything God wants to give through you. All you need to do is give of yourself and share your experience, lessons, and discoveries with them. Your job is not to make them like you but to help them become the person God created them to be—so that they may fulfill their purpose of obeying God.

ACTIVITIES

Ask God to reveal to you one person He wants you to invest in for the sole purpose of multiplying yourself. Maybe that person can be a child or a teenager, for Jesus said, "Let the little children come to me, and do not hinder them, for the kingdom of heaven belongs to such as these" (Matt. 19:14 NIV). It will require a commitment on your behalf, but that itself is part of your discipleship.

> *Dear Lord, You have blessed me and still are doing a great work in my heart. I pray that You send someone into my life who would willingly receive what You have to give them through me.*

HEROES

Meet Francisco at www.milesmcpherson.com.

Ph.DO

Become a mentor or start a mentoring program. To find out how, go to www.dosomethingworld.org.

DO Something! Myth 3

*I am not qualified to help
if I haven't experienced the pain
of those I am trying to help.*

The Lies Behind It

- People need our advice or experience.
- People only care about qualifications.
- Helping means fixing or having experience making things better.

The Truth

- People need our love. People care most about a willing heart.
- Helping is about being present with people who are hurting.

Scripture

Bear one another's burdens, and so fulfill the law of Christ.

—Galatians 6:2

Something to Remember

Your job is to be present and to hurt with those who are hurting.

Your presence and willingness to share the burden of those who are suffering is all that God has asked you to do.

Part 4

Pain

It Doesn't Have to Only Hurt

We all know that **pain** is inevitable, but we don't always realize that it can be turned into something powerful in our lives. Pain doesn't only have to hurt.

> No discipline seems pleasant at the time, but painful. Later on, however, it produces a harvest of righteousness and peace for those who have been trained by it.
>
> —Hebrews 12:11

16

Jordan

The Gift of Pain

My brethren, count it all joy when you fall into various trials, knowing that the testing of your faith produces patience. But let patience have its perfect work, that you may be perfect and complete, lacking nothing.

—James 1:2–4

The aroma of baking cookies crept upstairs and tickled Jordan's nose. The six-year-old dropped his bedtime book and peeked out of his door. No parents in sight, so he flew down the stairs in his SpongeBob pajamas. Nothing like fresh chocolate-chip cookies!

He yanked open the oven door and with his bare hands pulled the cookie sheet toward him, grabbing a handful of bubbling cookies. For the next few minutes, he stuffed his mouth with steaming dough, burning his fingers and lips and tongue.

He never felt the 350-degree heat or noticed the red blisters rising on his tongue and hands.

"Jordan!" yelled his mother, running into the kitchen.

· ·

Pain can do more than hurt; it can teach you the boundaries between right and wrong spiritual decisions.

Jesus looked out over the crowd stuffed shoulder to shoulder in the house. The sick, the lame, the poor, and the poor at heart were there, hoping for relief. Just as He started to resume His lesson on the kingdom of God, the sound of banging came from the ceiling. Dust and plaster fell on people's heads and shoulders, and they shielded their eyes as they looked up.

Suddenly a warm beam of sunlight pierced the dust and lit up Jesus, who must have started to smile. The crowd was murmuring. What was going on? Someone was ripping out a hole in the roof! More light flooded the room, and then was darkened by an odd shape.

Right above Jesus' head, a mat was being lowered by ropes, inch by inch, through the hole in the roof. On the mat was tied a bony man who couldn't move.

His four friends had seen him suffer long enough. They had nowhere else to turn, no one else to ask for help. They had heard what this Rabbi could do. The story recorded in Luke 5:17–19 says that, unfortunately, by the time they arrived at the house He was preaching in, an overflow crowd was busting out the front door. So they decided to go inside, like SWAT.

In what looked like something out of a *Rescue 911* show, four guys thought they would drop their paralytic friend in for some prayer.

Once the mat struck the floor, Jesus gave the disabled man something he probably wasn't expecting.

....

Jordan's mother snatched the remaining hot cookies out of Jordan's lap, tossed them on the counter, and poured cold water on a dishtowel. She gently wiped the chocolate off his face and fingers, and then wrapped his hands with the towel, all the while forcing herself not to scold him for being disobedient and injuring himself.

Jordan has a condition called CIPA: *congenital insensitivity to pain with anhidrosis*. He cannot feel pain or extreme temperatures.

CIPA is extremely rare. Only one in every 125 million suffer from it. That means Jordan is one of about three people in the entire United

States with this condition. When Jordan didn't cry as a newborn, the doctors—never imagining something like CIPA—just assumed he was a tough little guy.

To Jordan, a freezing cold day is no different from a sizzling summer day. Like every other adventurous boy who likes to jump off things, ride his bike in the street, play sports, and wrestle with his friends, Jordan is going to get hurt—but he will never feel it.

Unfortunately, whether he feels the pain or not, his body is still affected. Even though his lips, tongue, and throat couldn't feel the hot cookies, they still blistered.

Because of Jordan's condition, his parents, former NFL coach Tony Dungy and his wife, Lauren, need to watch him 24/7 as best they can. Because he cannot feel pain, he will never run to them for help, because he doesn't understand the need for help that pain is designed to show us.

Can you imagine, never knowing you had something as simple and common as a sprained ankle? You would keep walking on it, making the injury worse. The permanent damage would limit your ability to walk, dance, run, and jump for a lifetime.

The pain we feel is designed to protect us from harmful behavior. Without it we would continue to hurt ourselves.

....

God has given us pain to protect us, not only from physical harm, but from spiritual harm. Romans 6:23 tells us that *the penalty of sin is death*. Every time we sin, some level of death results.

How many times will you suffer the pain of violating God's standard of telling the truth before you stop telling lies?

How many times will you suffer the pain of sexual sin before you begin living in purity?

How many times will you endure the pain of disobedience to God until you learn the lessons that pain is trying to teach or the boundaries pain is trying to enforce?

God gave you pain to protect you from sin.

....

113

Four eager faces looked down through the hole in the ceiling. And as the paralyzed man twisted his head to look up at Jesus, Jesus saw their faith.

Jesus' reputation for healing people was one of the reasons the house was packed. But Jesus had a bigger fish to fry. He wanted to heal their broken spiritual condition.

Many people who come to God for physical healing or emotional relief are really suffering from spiritual CIPA. They do not realize how spiritually distant from God they really are.

The good news is that God sees your need and your faith.

Jesus looked at the paralytic and said, "Your sins are forgiven." He then told him to get up and walk, which he did, right out of the house, glorifying God as he went.

Pain is designed to bring you to the Father for help in time of need.

In fact, if you find yourself living a self-destructive life, it may be an indication that your relationship with God is distant—if it exists at all. The closer your relationship with God, the less self-destructive your life will be.

Sin brings physical, emotional, and spiritual pain—a reminder to avoid behavior that hurts not only us but God's heart as well.

Our responsibility is to allow our pain to bring us to Him for comfort.

Pain can do more than hurt; it can teach you the boundaries between right and wrong spiritual decisions. *And it can keep you from future mistakes.*

ACTIVITIES

Get together with or call a close friend. After explaining that you're reading this book and what this particular chapter is about, describe for your friend the pain you feel after you sin. Also explain (a) what you think your pain is teaching you to do and (b) what further pain your suffering may be protecting you from. Then invite your friend to share along similar lines.

Dear Lord, thank You for giving me the ability to feel pain, protecting me from my own sinfulness and long-term damage to my soul. Thank You, God, for all of the moral lessons I have learned about right and wrong through the painful experiences in my life.

HEROES

Hear Tony Dungy talking about his son, Jordan, at www.milesmcpherson.com.

17

Sherrill

Inside-Out Pain

And let us consider one another in order to stir up love and good works.

—Hebrews 10:24

Sherrill sat on a rusty stool in a shed behind her house. The thirty-nine-year-old waitress was holding a metal paint spatula under the blue flame of a propane torch until it was red-hot. But she wasn't working on a construction project.

She shut off the torch and rolled up her left sleeve. Scars covered the skin from her wrist to the inside of her elbow.

She had intentionally cut herself with razor blades and knives more times than she could remember. She had burned herself with heated tools and metal files, pressing them into her skin until she could no longer feel the pain.

Being molested for four years by her father had scarred her soul with so much self-hate, it had a mind of its own.

The only reason the molestation stopped was because her dad had a stroke that put him in a coma. But even after he died, Sherrill hated her body. It was the cause of too much pain. She resented being female. After all, if she had not been a girl, her dad would not have molested her—and she would not hurt like she did. She felt dirty and undeserving of anything good. Only pain.

When Sherrill was twelve, a girlfriend showed where she had carved the name of her boyfriend into her arm. The friend asked Sherrill to become her "blood sister," convincing her it wouldn't hurt and would be safe. They scratched their wrists with a razor and then pressed the bleeding wounds together.

Something about that pain made Sherrill feel free and powerful—for just a moment. That was the beginning of Sherrill's twenty-six years of "self-hurt" behavior.

In the kitchen she twirled the glowing spatula in her left hand until the large flat surface was pressed on the skin of her left forearm.

She wanted to blend all of the scars into one large one. But the real reason for such a painful act was deeper than that. It involved her very soul.

HELP *Wanted*

Approximately 1 percent of Americans, most of them women between the ages of thirteen and thirty, use "self-injury" to cope with overwhelming feelings or situations, according to research.[9]

. . . .

Jesus and His disciples walked toward the screams coming from tombs carved into a hill overlooking the Sea of Galilee. A skinny, naked man covered in scratches and scars stood pulling on the chain that tied his leg to a peg in the cave. Broken chains littered the mouth of the cave.

Suddenly the wild man arched his back and howled. Then he ran toward Jesus. The disciples stepped in front of their Lord, but the man fell at His feet first.

The demons that controlled him begged for mercy, saying, "What have I to do with You, Jesus, Son of the Most High God? I implore You by God that You do not torment me" (Mark 5:7).

Jesus spoke directly to the demons. "Come out of the man, unclean spirit!" He said (v. 8), and then

He ordered them into a herd of pigs that rushed off a cliff into the sea. The wild man was left sitting peacefully at the feet of Jesus. No more screaming. No more breaking chains or running around naked.

Instead of addressing the man's outward pain, his scars, and his wild behavior, Jesus spoke to the inner turmoil that was causing his pain.

....

Sherrill felt a sense of release as she pressed the red-hot spatula onto her arm. The smell of burning skin somehow represented pain escaping from her broken heart.

Sherrill's emotional pain was like a volcano in her heart. It had to come out at some point. She needed to find a diversion. The self-hurting through cutting and burning became that diversion.

The wounds, blood, and scars enabled Sherrill to give her inward pain an identity she could deal with. Without thinking it through logically, she had convinced herself that if she hurt herself, she could take control of the pain she was feeling and remove the power from the person who originally hurt her. The blood also gave her inward pain an external identity that she could relate to, that she could see and touch.

Internal pain not only hurts but also will attempt to become a self-inflicted external pain.

Sometimes her cutting experiences were close to suicide attempts, something like practice runs. But for the most part they were distractions from her inward pain. In her mind, it was a way to open herself and let the pain out.

People also inflict self-hurt when they feel guilty for doing something wrong or feel the shame that comes with the perception of *being* something wrong.

Life hurts sometimes, and the pain goes deep. Internal pain not only hurts but also will attempt to become self-inflicted external pain.

That self-hurt voice tells us to gossip, get drunk or high, go on an eating binge, or have sex. But fighting pain with pain never solves anything.

When Jesus saw the demon-possessed man, He did not address his physical outward pain, which was only a sign of his inward hurt. Instead He spoke directly to the source of the man's problems.

Jesus has a way of dealing directly with the pain we feel. He can apply His comfort directly to our inner scars and the trauma they cause. He can bring light into our life by revealing to us the real problem that is causing us to unnecessarily punish ourselves as an escape for what we or someone else has done to us.

It's time to let Jesus speak directly to your pain—dealing with the cause, and not the symptoms.

ACTIVITIES

Write down some unhealthy ways you escape from your pain. Through drinking? Cursing? Overeating? Now write down alternative ways to deal with pain. When you feel pain today, commit to doing something in the second list.

Dear Lord, please give me the compassion and insight to help lead my friends to a place where You can speak directly to the pain in their hearts. I also ask that You prepare their hearts for Your healing hand.

HEROES

Meet Sherrill at www.milesmcpherson.com.

Ph.DO

Begin a ministry or support group to help people with an eating disorder. For ideas, go to www. dosomethingworld.org.

119

18

Elisha

Exit Strategy

No temptation has overtaken you except such as is common to man; but God is faithful, who will not allow you to be tempted beyond what you are able, but with the temptation will also make the way of escape, that you may be able to bear it.

—1 Corinthians 10:13

Seven-year-old Elisha crawled into the back of his mother's car. He dropped his Spider-man backpack on the floor and flopped on the seat as if it was his bed.

He barely mumbled "hi."

From the front seat, Nova turned to ask, "What's wrong, Elisha?"

"I'm tired, Mom." He scratched his forehead through light-brown surfer hair that hung over his eyes.

"Why, honey?"

"There are so many kids at my school who got problems."

It's recess, a few hours earlier that same day. A hundred kids are swarming onto the playground, chattering and laughing.

In one corner of the blacktop, half a dozen first and second graders are in line. But they're not waiting their turn to play freeze tag or go down the slide. They're lining up for prayer.

At the front of the line, Elisha holds both hands of a first grader named Sheri. "What do you want me to pray for?"

"Grandma," Sheri whispers, eyes down. A tear drops on her pink Hannah Montana shirt. "She's got cancer. I heard Mom say she's gonna die."

Elisha prays, in his second-grader's language, for Sheri's grandma. "Dear Jesus, I pray for Sheri's grandma, that you would heal her so she would not get away from Jesus, the wrong way. I pray you put her into Jesus' heart. In Jesus' name, Amen."

A second-grade boy named Diego steps up next. Elisha asks what he wants prayer for.

"My dad. He needs a job," Diego says quietly.

Elisha prays for Diego's father.

A few more kids get in line. Ryan's brother is in jail. Tom has a cold. Susan's best friend is moving away and she's sad.

Elisha prays for them, one after another, until the bell rings.

With his shoulders slumped, he walks back to class to finish the day reading Dr. Seuss, exhausted from his pastoral duties.

All of this started because somebody told Elisha he wasn't cool.

....

A thin, sunburned Jesus walked out of the desert after his forty-day fast, and into a synagogue with His game face on.

It was normal for visiting rabbis to speak, so Jesus came expecting pulpit time.

The attendant of the synagogue pointed to the platform, handed Him a scroll containing the book of Isaiah the prophet. Jesus stepped to the podium, opened it, and read aloud.

> The Spirit of the LORD is upon Me,
> Because He has anointed Me
> To preach the gospel to the poor;

He has sent Me to heal the brokenhearted,
To proclaim liberty to the captives
And recovery of sight to the blind,
To set at liberty those who are oppressed;
To proclaim the acceptable year of the Lord.

Luke 4:18–19 (from Isaiah 61:1–2)

Everyone understood that this passage described the coming Messiah. But it was customary for rabbis to read a passage, and then sit down and explain it. So the men all stared at Jesus, wondering what He would say.

Jesus sat, looked around the room, and said the unthinkable: "Today this Scripture is fulfilled in your hearing" (Luke 4:21).

Their mouths dropped. They looked at one another. *Who does this guy think He is?* They started mumbling. "Isn't this Joseph's son?" (Luke 4:22 NIV).

Jesus knew what would happen, and He told them. He explained that the Messiah was going to give them foolproof evidence of His authority and power, and they would still reject Him. To make things worse, He said that the Gentiles would be the ones to accept and worship Him. In effect, He was saying, *You wouldn't know who the Messiah was if He hit you on the head.*

They went ballistic. *They* were God's chosen people, not the Gentiles.

Tearing their clothes and beating their chests, they cried out, "He must die!" Screaming "Blasphemy!" they pushed and shoved Jesus like an angry mob of paparazzi. They got Him out where they could throw him off a three-story cliff. That would put a stop to this madman's delusions of grandeur.

Somehow amidst the screaming, scrambling, fist pumping, and chest beating, Jesus simply walked through the crowd and went about His Father's business.

The whole commotion was caused by a conflict over Jesus' identity. He claimed to be God. They labeled Him a blasphemer. Jesus was committed to who He was—not who the crowd was trying to define Him to be.

We must first be committed to who we are, the people God made us to be. You cannot let pain, or the people and circumstances causing your pain, define you. *If we remain committed to who we are in spite of the pains of life that come our way, we will walk through them and do something significant in the world.*

....

When you experience pain, you have two response options. They are both directly related to how you define yourself.

First, you can allow the negative nature of pain caused by rejection, tragedy, or misfortune to define you as weak, as a failure, or as not good enough. This was Satan's accusation about Job; this was the claim of the men Jesus faced in the synagogue. If you choose to allow pain to redefine you in these terms, you will probably not see God's exit strategy. Even if someone walked up to you with God's solution, you wouldn't believe it would work. You already have accepted the label of loser.

The second potential response to pain is to define yourself as a courageous victor by identifying yourself as belonging to God. You can acknowledge that He loves you and has never forgotten you. You can label yourself as someone who is in the middle of a lesson that involves pain as a tool to sharpen your reliance on the Lord.

If that is who you are, God's exit strategy will be clearer to you.

Because Jesus knew exactly who He was and was aware of the plan associated with His identity, He knew that death by "cliff crash" was not how He would "go out."

However, though Jesus took advantage of a divine exit strategy and walked away from the cliff and the mob that screamed blasphemy, He did not walk away from the mob that cried out "Crucify Him!" (John 19:6). Being crucified was part of His fulfilling the purpose of His identity.

HELP
Wanted

Bullying is widespread in American schools, with more than 16 percent of children saying they had been bullied by other students, according to a survey funded by the National Institute of Child Health and Human Development (NICHD).[19]

Knowing who you are will not protect you from ever being hurt by pain. But it will ensure that pain doesn't *only* hurt. It will allow you to take advantage of God's exit strategy for you. Remember, even though Jesus died, He still had an exit strategy: His resurrection.

Are you a child of God, or not? Did God give you a clear purpose with a plan and all of the necessary preparations made for you to succeed in that plan? Yes! Therefore, no matter what pain you experience, hold on to who God made you and look to Him for how to respond.

....

Little Elisha was already the campus MOG—man of God. During the Christmas season the students were asked to describe what they thought Saint Nick looked like. One response said, "Just like Elisha." Another time kids were asked to answer the question, "What would you ask of God if you came face to face with God?" One replied, "I'd have to talk with Elisha first."

Nevertheless, not everyone was impressed by his John the Baptist–like identity.

A few weeks before Elisha stood praying for his friends, during a different recess period, Elisha had walked over to three second graders he knew standing together on the playground. "What's going on?" he asked.

"We're starting a Cool Club," said one of the boys.

"And you can't be in it," said another.

"Yeah, you're not cool enough," said the third.

As far as they were concerned, he was a Cool Club reject.

However, whether Elisha was a reject or not wasn't their decision, but Elisha's. Whether this painful situation would stay painful was not their decision, but Elisha's.

Was he an uncool victim of their childish games, or a child of God?

When Elisha was rejected by the Cool Club kids, he had a choice to make.

The next day at lunchtime, he yelled so that everyone on the playground could hear him. "Hey, everyone! It's Bible Club time and everyone is welcome."

Elisha was fired up. This seven-year-old was going to preach the gospel on his little campus.

On the first day, only six kids "joined" the Bible Club. But some of them came back the next time and brought their friends. Then ten kids sat in the schoolyard and listened to Elisha's lesson.

The next time, thirty kids came.

The group got so big that the school employee who oversees recess let Elisha borrow a megaphone. Every week now, Elisha sits on the lunch table while thirty to fifty kids listen to his Bible study.

God is always confident you can find the exit strategy He has for you. But you have to be willing to look for it and act on it.

God promises never to allow you to be tested beyond what you can bear (1 Cor. 10:13). If you will make the decision to not allow pain to redefine you, God's exit strategy will be staring you in the face.

After all, God does not create an escape route toward failure. Satan has already taken care of that. For example, if you want to drink your way out of your problems, that is the devil's option.

And the devil's options lead to more pain and self-destruction.

•••

It was after one of these Bible Club meetings when the lunch attendant asked if anyone wanted Elisha to pray for them specifically. That's how those seven kids ended up in the line and how Elisha ended up laid out in the backseat of his mom's van.

If you are in a painful situation today, do something about defining who you are: victim or victor.

If you are a victor, God has an exit strategy for you, and all you need to do is walk through it.

ACTIVITIES

Choose a painful situation you are going through and ask yourself, how is my pain trying to redefine me? Compare that label to who the Bible says Christians are, such as members of the body of Christ (1 Cor. 12:13), a holy priesthood (1 Peter 2:9), Jesus' brothers and sisters (Mark 3:35). Now, based on your biblical identity, write down how you will respond to the pain.

Dear God, I am Your child. Please show me how a child who trusts in You with their whole heart would respond to my trial. Please give me the direction I need. Help me with my response to pain and align it to my "God identity."

HEROES

Meet Elisha at www.milesmcpherson.com.

Ph.DO

To help start an elementary school ministry like Elisha did, go to www.dosomethingworld.org.

19

Doc

Your Painful Opportunity

But sanctify the Lord God in your hearts, and always be ready to give a defense to everyone who asks you a reason for the hope that is in you, with meekness and fear.

—1 Peter 3:15

The linebacker called "34 cover two free" and we all said "Break!" I started licking my lips and rubbing my hands together. I loved this defense.

The silver and black Raiders, our number one rival, jogged to the line of scrimmage. We screamed "Left! Left!" to signal that their tight end lined up on our left. Once they broke their huddle and lined up, we started walking back and forth yelling our audibles, changing the play. It could actually change two or three times before the ball was snapped. *Sky, Sky, left, right, check 2, Lucy!* We had about thirty plays on defense in our own language.

As a safety, my job was to defend against the deep passes down the field. I spent most of my time covering either in the deep middle third of the field or the left or right half of the field. Where I was on the field was one of the first things the quarterback looked for. Once he spotted me, he would begin trying to figure out what kind of defense we were in and where he might throw the ball. But it was still early. A lot would happen between breaking the huddle and the end of the play.

The center snapped the ball. I immediately turned and ran away from the QB to cover the deep half of the field. "Cover two free" was a disguised "two deep" coverage. I was going to make him think that the middle would be wide open. Once I was convinced the QB thought I was going to the deep left half of the field, I ducked and ran back toward him into the shallow middle, hiding behind the 300-pound linemen up front. The plan was to bait him into throwing across the middle, right where I was planning to be in about one second, before he could blink.

Then, *here comes Christmas!* As I ran toward the QB to my zone—in the middle of the field to about ten yards from the line of scrimmage—here came the ball, a little high, but right at me.

Oh boy, it's *Monday Night Football*—my first as a starter for the San Diego Chargers—and players from all over the NFL, my family, all the "fellas" at home are watching. *There's nothing but green in between me and the end zone.*

Up I went for what felt like thirty feet. The ball came spinning toward me. I had seen this a thousand times and caught this a thousand times. Then, just as the ball touched my fingertips, something as hard as a rock wrapped around my knee. Spun into a cartwheel, I went around and down.

• •

Along the bumpy cobblestone road in Jerusalem, screaming crowds kept bumping each other as they lined both sides. Some of the people cursed at Jesus. Others were weeping, feeling the pain of His beating themselves. They were the ones who loved Him.

Bent over from the weight of the heavy cross, Jesus spent most of the half-mile walk to His death facing the ground, where His blood and saliva dripped onto the stone pavement. The cross bounced on His shredded back as it dragged on the uneven stone road. The mob roared every time a Roman soldier's whip ripped skin from His back.

Exhausted, He fell.

Grabbing a random man from the crowd, a soldier forced a guy named Simon to carry the cross while Jesus struggled to get up.

Those who loved Him screamed for mercy, but Jesus turned and encouraged them. "Daughters of Jerusalem, do not weep for Me" (Luke 23:28).

Don't cry for Me, Jesus was saying. *I will be in heaven in a few hours. This blood and these wounds may seem bad to you right now, but they're going to lead to a blessing for you, if you trust Me. You all need to beware of the coming judgment, because* that *is going to be a lot worse for you than this pain is for Me.*

"Mission accomplished" was waiting for Him at the top of the hill. What looked like agony to the crowd was actually a victory lap. Jesus wanted no pity party. He was fully confident that God had provided for Him the strength not only to prevail but to minister in the midst of pain.

The most important thing for Him to do was to be obedient to whatever God had called Him to do, even amidst His suffering.

Your eternal purpose to *obey God* does not take a time-out during your suffering.

Look for opportunities to minister during your pain. The hope expressed by someone crying is the most powerful hope. The comfort shared by someone who is uncomfortable can be the most life-changing comfort. It is during your time of suffering that, more than ever, you will cry out to God. It is the joy resulting from that cry that is most purely God's.

God intends to use unique opportunities to express Himself through you at a time when you are most dependent on Him.

The next time you are suffering, in pain, being persecuted, look around and ask God, "Is there someone You want me to encourage? Is there someone I am to model graceful suffering to?"

Be confident that the comfort and encouragement God gives you is intended for you *and* for anyone He sends your way. He wants the overflow of His love in your life to fall onto as many people as possible.

But this can only happen if you take your eyes off feeling sorry for yourself and turn them toward blessing someone else.

I looked the team doctor in the eye. "My career ended tonight, Doc. You know that, don't you?"

Dr. Losse and I were on the Chargers team bus, rumbling down Interstate 5 from Los Angeles after our game against the Raiders. In my head, I could still hear the 90,000 Raider fans screaming. Our pass defense was one of the best in the league after three games, and the LA Coliseum was a great place to "do our thang." As a former Division III football player, this had been a big night for me. A dream come true—one that would prove all my critics wrong.

But it didn't turn out the way I dreamed it would.

Sitting next to the team physician made it official. I was his next surgery for sure. Dr. Losse—it's pronounced *low-see*, not *loss*, by the way—was already caring for his patient.

The sledgehammer that ruined my interception and shattered my football career was simply a cast on the arm of my own 6-foot-4, 240-pound linebacker running in the wrong direction.

My own teammate blew out my knee.

Up, over, and down I had gone. As my feet flipped over my head, I thought, *What in the world hit me?*

By the time I landed, I knew the hit had ruined more than the interception. My knee felt wrong. Pain mixed with the sensation of things on the inside of my leg being in the wrong place. Everything was just wrong.

This cannot be happening. This cannot be happening . . .

I immediately began thinking about how soon I would be able to get back in the game. But the longer I laid there, for seconds that seemed like minutes, the more I knew what was next. Surgery, weeks of being out, everything I had worked for and earned to that point, lost.

The game went on. As I sat alone on the bench, guys came over one by one and patted me on the shoulder. The very next play, a teammate made the play I thought I was going to make, an interception for a touchdown. *That was supposed to be me.*

So that's how I ended up on the bus next to the doctor, with five pounds of ice on my leg and an Ace bandage wrapped from mid-thigh to mid-calf, thinking about the beginning of the end.

Having come to the Chargers as a free agent, I felt like I had one shot to establish myself. In fact, I had replaced a ten-year veteran, who stepped back into his position when I got hurt. After all, the only way I made it to the NFL was by the grace of God. According to the NFL, of the 8,500 players drafted since 1980, only 378 were from a Division II school. This is about 4 percent. God gave me the talent, the health, and the opportunity to enable me to play the game.

But He did not create me just to play football. He had other plans.

I was good with that. In theory. My problem with my ripped-up knee was a timing issue. I wasn't ready to begin the transition yet.

But there was nothing I could do about it. This wasn't about me, either—it was about God. Complaining was not going to make my knee better. If anything, it would slow down the healing process.

It was time for me to put my faith into practice. Everyone knew I was a Christian. I'm sure someone on that bus was thinking, *So where was your God tonight? He didn't do a very good job of keeping you healthy, did He?*

But God never promised to keep me healthy. He promised to bless me with His peace if I was obedient in all circumstances. Now was the time for me to be obedient and to minister out of my pain.

So the million-dollar question was: how would I handle it?

Would I complain to God for ruining the best night of my life? Or would I recognize the opportunity I had? The doctor was trapped in the window seat with nothing to do but listen to me. And I certainly wasn't going anywhere.

Well, I'm no saint, but I saw an opportunity that my pain had provided.

For two hours I shared with Doc how much God loved him. I told him about what God had done in my life. I shared that in the last two years I was cut by the Los Angeles Rams and found myself with no job and no idea of what would happen to my life. Then I was invited to a private tryout with the Chargers, along with two other players who also had been cut by the Rams. I was signed on to the team, got involved with the wrong crowd, and started using cocaine. The head of the team security knew I was getting high and was just about to arrest me when I stopped using and began going to church. God has always been there for me through all of my ups and downs.

This injury was just another opportunity for God to prove His faithfulness. "Doc, I know that this is probably the end of my opportunity on this team." He nodded because he knew what the politics on a team can be like. "But because of all God has done for me over the years, I know He will continue to take care of me."

The doc listened and nodded, although he did not make a decision that night to follow Christ. But that was okay. My responsibility was to lovingly share with him the hope I had.

I was charged to do something obedient, even amidst my pain, and that's what I did.

ACTIVITIES

Today, go to your local hospital and sit in the lobby. Pray for the people you see there; try to be an encouragement to them somehow. Then pray that if you were ever to end up there in pain that God would give you the strength to minister to those around you. Remember, some of our best opportunities to heal those around us are when we are in a vulnerable place.

Dear Lord, the next time I am in pain, being ridiculed or frustrated, I ask that You show me who You want me to be a model sufferer for. I pray that I would have the maturity to share the hope of Your comfort with others even while I am still hurting. And please give me the strength to be an encouragement to those who are trying to encourage me.

20

David

The Equalizer

But if you suffer for doing good and you endure it, this is commendable before God. To this you were called, because Christ suffered for you, leaving you an example, that you should follow in his steps.

—1 Peter 2:20–21 NIV

"Get off the roof! Get off the roof!"

David heard the captain yelling at him and his rookie partner, Rio, from below. They were on top of a burning million-dollar house in Hollywood Hills, cutting holes in the roofing to act as vents for the fire and smoke. The flashing red lights from the seven trucks popped through the white smoke and reflected off their yellow turnout gear and oxygen masks.

The first hole was drawing out a good amount of fire, so David decided to enlarge it. Meanwhile, Rio had crept down a sloped section of the roof to cut a second hole.

Then David heard the crack of splintering wood. Spinning around, David saw Rio fall through the imploding roof as a ball of fire exploded out of the opening. In the next second, Rio's head and shoulders popped up above the hole in the roof as flames shot up all around him. David scrambled over and dove to grab Rio—and the roofing under his own feet caved in. Now his legs dangled between roof beams in the flames. With a handful of the back of Rio's coat, David didn't know what to do.

"Help!"

....

When you suffer on behalf of others in Jesus' name, it will hurt, but know this: this pain, more than anything else, makes you like Jesus.

As everyone around the table was talking and eating, Jesus lifted a large piece of unleavened bread, and the second-floor banquet room got quiet. On the table was Jesus' last meal with His disciples.

The twelve disciples watched Him grasp the bread with both hands and tear it in two. Extending both arms, He passed one piece to His left and one to His right. Slowly each disciple broke off a small chunk.

"This is My body which is given for you," Jesus then said. "Do this in remembrance of Me" (Luke 22:19).

He had already told them He was going to suffer and die. Now He was showing them, teaching them, what His death would mean.

His companions' eyes stayed glued on Him as they quietly chewed their bread.

Then Jesus lifted a cup of wine, motioned to both sides of the table, and drank from it. Next He poured half of the remainder into two other ceramic cups, passing them to both sides of the table.

"This cup is the new covenant in My blood, which is shed for you," he said (v. 20).

Jesus' message to them was simple: *My body is going to be ripped. My blood will be shed. And I am doing it for anyone who will believe in Me.*

Glancing left and right, Jesus paused. Did the disciples understand the message?

"Do this in remembrance of Me," He said. Whenever they thought of Him, He wanted them to think of the broken bread and the wine.

Whenever you mention My name, think of My ripped flesh, My spilled blood.

When you think of Me, the first thought I want to come into your mind is of the pain I endured on behalf of those I love.

I will have died so that others have the opportunity to live.

When you suffer on behalf of others in Jesus' name, it will hurt, but know this: this pain, more than anything else, makes you like Jesus.

Jesus embraced pain on behalf of the world. So should we.

HELP *Wanted*

According to the United States Fire Administration, 114 firefighters died while on duty in 2008.[11]

Two firefighters scrambled up and lunged at David, grabbing his free arm and the oxygen tank on his back. They couldn't get to Rio from their position. The blaze was too hot and intense.

The other men pulled on David as David kept his grip on the shoulder of Rio's turnout jacket. Rio was facing away from them, but they all knew that the more than 1000-degree heat engulfing him was pushing the limits of his fire resistant clothing. Through the flame and smoke, David stared at the back of Rio's helmet, praying that the roof would hold for just a minute more.

But then he realized he had another problem. His hand was burning. The flames that shot up four feet above Rio's head were also cooking David's hand. He could have easily justified letting go, but then Rio would die.

He kept telling himself, *Don't let go! He's going to die! Don't let go!*

Just in time, a fifth fireman climbed onto the roof from the opposite side and yanked Rio out of his hole.

Both David and Rio suffered second- and third-degree burns on their arms, legs, and feet. But the most significant burn was on the hand that would not let go of Rio's coat.

It was the hand that was willing to suffer to save Rio's life.

···

The Bible tells us to "bear one another's burdens, and so fulfill the law of Christ" (Gal. 6:2). This doesn't apply only when it feels good. Anyone can do that. We are most like Jesus when we bear someone's burden beyond what's comfortable and convenient, even beyond what's safe.

Jesus' willingness to allow Himself to be beaten, spit on, slapped, whipped, and nailed to the cross on our behalf gave us the opportunity to avoid the eternal punishment our sins deserve. The only reason we have an opportunity to have eternal life is because of the suffering Jesus endured on our behalf.

If we are going to do something like Jesus, we must be willing to suffer on behalf of someone else, giving them the opportunity to avoid unnecessary pain in their lives. There will be opportunities to sacrifice your time or money to help someone get back on their feet. You may need to go into a dangerous part of town or have a hard conversation in order for someone to experience the love of God. Your being inconvenienced on behalf of someone once or twice may save them from a lifetime of the pain that comes from bad decisions.

The difference between someone being saved from the fire may be not only your ability to suffer but the *length and degree* to which you can suffer on that person's behalf.

One definition of *patience* is longsuffering. It can come in the form of something as dramatic as holding onto someone while your hand is burning, or as simple as sacrificing your TV time to sit up all night to pray with a suicidal friend.

If you are living to avoid pain, you will undoubtedly limit yourself in what you do in God's service. The difference between heaven and hell is not Jesus' wisdom or His miracles or His gentle spirit. Yes, he had all of those. But what really saves us is the incredibly painful death He suffered on our behalf.

Never discount the eternal impact your suffering can have on the person you are inconvenienced for.

ACTIVITIES

Go through some amount of pain or discomfort to be of help to someone in need. Sign up for a run that benefits people who are suffering. Give more than you usually do to church or to a worthwhile charity. Shatter your comfort zone by taking a homeless person out to eat. As you do it, pray for that person or those people.

Dear Lord, please send someone into my path today whose burden I can help carry. Please reveal to me my selfishness—the part of me that avoids identifying with Jesus' discomfort on behalf of other people—and help me overcome it.

HEROES

Meet David at www.milesmcpherson.com.

Ph.DO

Start a ministry to firefighters in your community. For ideas, go to www.dosomethingworld.org.

DO Something! Myth 4

I need to wait to do something until

(1) I have learned more,

(2) I have grown more, or

(3) I am all done hurting.

The Lies behind It

- God can't use us until we are "done" maturing in Him.
- *Doing something* is only the result of growth, not the mechanism for growth.
- We have to be perfect and "whole" to be used by God.

The Truth

The ministry opportunities God has prepared for us not only build His kingdom, they also serve to grow us up in Him. *Doing something* is one of the processes God uses to mature our faith and heal our brokenness and pain.

Scripture

Now no chastening seems to be joyful for the present, but painful; nevertheless, afterward it yields the peaceable fruit of righteousness to those who have been trained by it.
—Hebrews 12:11

Something to Remember

Doing something is what you do throughout your whole life walking with God.

It is not the result of what you've learned from Him, it's how you learn it.

It's okay to make mistakes. You don't have to be perfect. You just have to be available and obedient.

Part 5

Power

The Ability to DO

There are two kinds of **power** available to you: natural and supernatural.

You will only be able to do the "greater works" Jesus talked about if you use His supernatural power, which has the ability to reach down into the natural world and supersede anything that natural power can attempt to do.

> Now to Him who is able to do exceedingly abundantly above all that we ask or think, according to the power that works in us.
>
> — Ephesians 3:20

21

Jessica

The Strength of Surrender

And being found in appearance as a man, He humbled Himself and became obedient to the point of death, even the death of the cross. Therefore God also has highly exalted Him and given Him the name which is above every name, that at the name of Jesus every knee should bow, of those in heaven, and of those on earth, and of those under the earth, and that every tongue should confess that Jesus Christ is Lord, to the glory of God the Father.

—Philippians 2:8–11

As Tom's hand squeezed her throat, Jessica endured the worst five minutes of her life on the floor, in and out of consciousness. Slapping her, ripping her clothes, pinning her leg to the cheap carpet with his knee, her ex-husband tried to strip Jessica of every last bit of self-esteem—so that he could feel powerful.

"There was no one on the earth weaker than me," she recalls. For years she had lived in complete fear—defeated and under the control of an evil man. That's how she had felt meeting Tom that day for a long-overdue payment of child support.

But in those awful minutes struggling against her attacker, every-thing changed for Jessica. Amidst her weakness, she became strong. Looking back on the rape, she now realizes that stumbling to her car and making her way to the police station was the beginning of her gaining her own power back.

Jessica may have walked out of the house covered in blood and bruises, but she was full of confidence. It doesn't happen that way for all women who go through such trauma. But Jessica realized that her worst nightmare had not destroyed her. Her greatest fear had not defeated her. Thus, there was no reason to fear it anymore.

"At that moment," she says now, looking back, "I made a deliberate decision that I'd never go through this again, and neither would my son. I told myself I was no longer a victim. I became a survivor."

There is nothing more powerful than a person with nothing to lose and everything to gain. Jessica's pain had turned into power.

· ·

Jesus' actions on earth were miraculous, supernatural, and often unexplainable. The question is, how did He get so much power in the first place? We are called to live a supernatural life as well; how are we to tap God's power in our lives?

I define *power* as the ability to move obstacles, both physical and nonphysical. When obstacles are moved, we are free to do whatever God has called us to do.

Because the "do somethings" that God has prepared you for are spiritual in nature, the most important obstacles to move are those things that inhibit you from fulfilling God's purpose in your life. Those obstacles can be moved only by spiritual power.

Spiritual power is not gained in the same manner as human power. Human power is often taken by force and at the expense of another person. Tom "proved" his strength by doing something horrible to Jessica that she was not able to stop. By overcoming her power, he was essentially taking it for himself.

God's supernatural power, on the other hand, can only come from God and is never taken from Him.

When Jesus humbled Himself and became a man, His deity was voluntarily surrendered, being covered in human likeness. He set aside the heavenly glory He had with the Father from before the

142

foundation of the world. He allowed sinners to betray, beat, and eventually crucify Him.

The crowds mocked Him, thinking they were exercising their power by overcoming His self-proclaimed deity. They challenged Him to prove His power by coming down off the cross.

Little did they realize that His act of self-surrender was how He secured the highest level of power and authority for Himself. He allowed religious leaders to slap Him, Pilate to judge Him, and Roman soldiers to nail Him on the cross. For this reason, His name was exalted above every other name.

HELP *Wanted*

Every two minutes in the United States, someone is sexually assaulted.[12]

．．

The Bible says humility comes before honor, and pride comes before a fall. It was in the midst of Jessica's rape that she became strong. The newfound determination came as a result of what Tom did to her. With it came an opportunity that turned into power.

We will live powerless lives when we feel the need to put others down to lift ourselves up. It is twice as cowardly when we tear people down behind their backs, when they cannot defend themselves.

God's power comes when you stop trying to take power from other people and allow yourself to receive it from God.

God's power comes when you surrender your desires and plans to the almighty loving God and pursue what He wants for your life.

God's power comes when you can surrender your interests and begin to act on behalf of others instead of at the expense of others.

Jessica's healing process is ongoing. At first she blamed God for not preventing her tragedy. But she also remembers thinking that day that she easily could have died.

Her ex-husband is now serving a twenty-nine-year prison sentence. She now thanks God, not only for her life, but for being able to sit on her porch with a book without wondering who is spying on her from the car across the street. She is thankful for being able to go grocery shopping without jumping every time someone walks up behind her. Her surrendering to God has helped her reorder her priorities. She lives a simpler life, focused on God's plans and not her own.

One of the first acts of power that Jessica exercised was to produce a PowerPoint presentation for teens who have experienced abuse or might be vulnerable to it. She also started a ministry to victims of domestic violence at the Rock Church.

Jessica converted the comfort she received into the comfort she could give. She converted the painful lessons she learned into insights she taught. Young girls have told her they are living her nightmare; helping them has given her life a powerful purpose.

So stop trying to take power from people and begin receiving it from God. Do something about surrendering your will to Him on His terms.

ACTIVITIES

Identify one example of taking power from someone else by tearing him or her down. This could be by gossiping or backbiting, actively preventing them from being blessed, taking credit for doing something when you shouldn't, and so on.

Dear Lord, please reveal to me the way I am trying to take power from someone else. How am I trying to make myself feel strong by putting someone else down? Please, God, empower me today to humble myself before You, and to trust that You will bless me with all of the power I need if I only obey You.

HEROES

Meet Jessica at www.milesmcpherson.com.

_Ph.DO_

Start a ministry to those involved in domestic violence, as Jessica did. For tips on how to do this, go to www.dosomethingworld.org.

22

Miles

God's Fingerprint

Whether He is a sinner or not I do not know. One thing I know: that though I was blind, now I see.

—John 9:25

Sweat soaked through my T-shirt and shorts. My heart was going crazy in my chest—like I was at the peak of a workout. But I wasn't.

I was in my living room, trying to sleep after another night of cocaine. Sleep and cocaine? I don't think so.

The dark room felt like an oven. A thin beam of sunlight shot through the drawn blinds and hit my face. My eyes felt propped open, dry. My blurry vision was dark around the corners, except for tiny bursts of sparkle, like glitter in the dirt. My muscles ached. I tried to lift my arms, but they were glued to my chest.

Yet my heart sprinted. A fellow NFL player had recently died from a cocaine-induced cardiac arrest. I was scared. But tired too. Really tired. *Please let me sleep*. I was sick of the bare beige walls I had stared at all night. I was sick of the suffocating new-furniture smell of my cream-colored sectional. I was sick of the lies I lived by. I was sick of the dark side of my life.

How could I be this close to letting stupidity kill me?

I play professional football. I am twenty-four years old. I am living the dream. What is my problem?

I had bought a little white matchbook-sized package of cocaine to last me the night as I studied for the anatomy class I was taking at San Diego State University during the off-season. But was my life really what I wanted it to be? I was stuck in an ugly pattern of cocaine use.

It was now 5:00 a.m. I had finished studying and found myself wide awake, alone, and thinking about my life.

Five years had gone by since encountering the hippies in that TSS store in New York. Their long hair and beards never left my mind. Neither did the memory of what we spoke about. Specifically, the commitment I made to Jesus. A commitment I hadn't kept.

The image of Jesus standing in my girlfriend's mother's room was also fresh in my mind half a decade later.

I had created so much drama in my life since then, partying, getting high, using girls, going to crack houses, and putting football before God. Were the hippies right? Did Jesus still love me? Or had He given up on me?

There I was, between my second and hopefully third year in the NFL. Theoretically, God couldn't possibly have made my life better. I was a pro football player. I was single. I got high whenever I wanted. I partied whenever I felt like it.

During the season I played football six days per week. Went to practice five days a week. Morning meetings, watching film and studying the next opponent. Then lunch with the team, followed by a workout and then a two-hour practice. Then, game day. Lights, cameras, and action. The following day was a half day, which consisted of watching film of the game and a light workout, and then our one day off. Week in, week out.

All that sounded good. But the bottom line was, I was living the life of a fool. I had the coaches fooled, the media fooled, my girlfriend and family fooled. But the saddest thing about it, I had fooled myself into thinking that my life was working. I had fooled myself into thinking that I was actually having fun.

It is one thing to be discouraged when everything in your life is falling apart. But how do you explain being unhappy when fulfilled dreams don't satisfy? Where do you go then?

If I keep doing what I am doing, I thought that bitter morning in April, *where am I going to end up?*

After lying on that couch all night, I decided enough was enough.

There has to come a time in your life that you are willing to completely surrender everything to God.

....

As Jesus walked with His disciples past a crowd of beggars on the road, He saw a guy who had been blind since birth.

Jesus squatted down, spat on the ground, and began to make mud with His saliva. The guy might have been blind, but his ears worked fine. "Will somebody please tell me what He is doing?" he called out.

Everyone was thinking, *You don't want to know,* but no one said anything. Jesus rubbed the dirt and saliva between His hands, placed the mud on the eyes of the blind man, and told him to wash his face in the Pool of Siloam. The pool was spring water that flowed into the city from an underground spring. It was considered to be pure and have healing powers.

"Take me to the pool!" the man demanded of his friend, and grabbed his hand. Feeling his way down the steps to the water, he fell onto his stomach to splash his face and rub off the mud. Then he jerked his head out of the water. He looked at his friend, he looked at other sick people in the water, he looked up at the sun, and he started screaming. For the first time in his life, he could see.

The blind man's neighbors immediately took him to the Pharisees, the religious leaders who resented Jesus. Every chance these religious leaders got they tried to discredit Jesus. But this time, what would they say about a blind man receiving his sight? How could they deny that?

When the blind man explained that Jesus made mud with His spit and healed him, their only reply was, it was the wrong day of the week to heal someone. And because it was the wrong day, He must not be from God. "This Man is not from God, because He does not keep the Sabbath" (John 9:16).

Of course God only works on certain days. Right? Not! Those guys couldn't heal a blind man no matter what day of the week it was.

But the one thing they couldn't deny was what the formerly blind man said. "Whether He is a sinner or not I do not know. One thing I know: that though I was blind, now I see" (John 9:25).

· ·

When the hippies had confronted me, I remember sensing Jesus in that store. About a week later, the Lord had appeared to me while I lay in my girlfriend's mother's bed.

Five years had passed since then. During that half hour or so when I sat in the crack house bathroom staring at "the cook," I knew Jesus was nudging me to love him.

Jesus had been calling me for years, asking me to give Him an honest chance to change my life.

I finally got it. On April 12, 1984, at about 5:00 a.m., I had enough.

I told God I was not going to fight Him any longer. I belonged to Him. I made a decision that morning to obey God with my life. Lying on the couch that day, it was time for me to surrender and stay surrendered.

That day was the end of my getting high, getting drunk, and cursing. My girlfriend and I got back together, and we vowed to be celibate until the night we got married, which we did five months later.

No more clubbing, no more hanging out with my "we-are-professional-sinners" friends who would drag me down. I started going to the team Bible studies and hanging out with a few of the married couples on the team.

That day I fully acknowledged my commitment to God. I was ready to walk with Him.

Can you point to a miracle in your life that God has performed that is undeniably evidence of His power in your life?

HELP
Wanted

An estimated 23 million Americans are addicted to alcohol or other substances.[13]

Can you say in one way or another, *I was blind and now I see?*

Nothing will validate the power of God in your life more than the power of God being displayed in and through your life. When Jesus was accused of casting out demons by the power of the devil, He said, "But if I cast out demons with the finger of God, surely the kingdom of God has come upon you" (Luke 11:20).

I was addicted and now I am sober. I was an angry, promiscuous, violent God-hater, and now I am free.

What has God done that no amount of your own willpower can get the credit for?

What has God done that no amount of discipline can claim it has done?

Don't get me wrong. Discipline and willpower are necessary. Just not enough. After all, when you share God's love with someone, you are claiming that He has the power to change your life from the inside out. If you have not experienced that power, what are your claims based on?

There will be people who claim to know God, but their lives will lack evidence of His power. They will have a form of godliness but deny its power (2 Tim. 3:2–5).

Keep in mind, God is in the life-transforming business. He's looking for people who are willing to change and even desperate for a change. I was "done" with what drugs were doing to me. I was tired of sneaking around, wasting my money, and living a lie. Is there any area of your life that you are fed up with?

Be honest with God about it. Tell Him you need His power and ask Him to send change your way. His power may come in the form of a willingness to get counseling, a decision to delete phone numbers, or a desire to pray more. But know this, you will need to do something, probably more than once. It will most likely take time. And you will need to do what He tells you.

Whether or not you realize it, God has already worked supernaturally in your life. If you think back to the most desperate times in your life, it was probably God who got you through it. Or what over-the-top opportunities does God deserve the credit for?

These are evidence that God has been faithful in your life, and that He will continue to be faithful in your future.

Instead of focusing on the obstacles you will always be confronted with, look for proof of God's power.

ACTIVITIES

Develop a sixty-second testimony of your own "I-was-blind-now-I-see" story. How have you experienced the power of God in your life?

Dear Jesus, I want to experience a double dose of Your power in my life, not for my benefit but for Your benefit. I want to be radically transformed into who You want me to be. Reveal to me one area that needs Your transforming power the most, and give me the courage to surrender it to You. Please display Your power in that area in such a way that even Your critics will give You credit.

Ph.DO

For tips on how to share your testimony go to www.dosomethingworld.org.

23

Tamela

Pay It Forward

Blessed be the God and Father of our Lord Jesus Christ, the Father of mercies and God of all comfort, who comforts us in all our tribulation.

—2 Corinthians 1:3–4

"It's gone! I think it's gone! Honey! Honey!"

Tamela had jumped out of the shower and was dripping on the bathroom floor, staring at her sternum. Now she ran downstairs to the kitchen, where her husband, Major, was fixing breakfast. He looked up, surprised. "Tam?"

"I'm healed! I'm healed!" she cried, dancing around Major, not caring that she didn't have a stitch of clothing on. "Look! The lump is gone! Call the doctor!"

Major examined Tamela's chest. Yes, the grapefruit-sized tumor between her breasts was gone. In its place was a bump of bone. "I think it is, Tam. It *is* gone."

Memories flooded Tamela's mind as Major went to grab a blanket off the couch to wrap her in.

Tamela was one of those super moms. She had two master's degrees, one in organizational management and another in business administration. She had just signed a lease on a commercial kitchen to service her soul-food catering business. And she was homeschooling her five-year-old daughter.

She had discovered the hard lump on her chest a year ago, at the beginning of her last pregnancy. It didn't hurt, and her doctor told her they would check it monthly. But as soon as her second daughter was born, her doctor ordered tests.

She remembered entering the beige and pea-green medical offices with her mother to hear the results. She wondered why one of the doors said *Infusion/Chemo*, and why the reception area was full of bald, sick-looking people.

When Dr. Redfern, a tall, blond man with blue eyes in a boyish face, broke the news, she said that it "felt like I was hit by a train but still standing."

Dr. Redfern explained she had a form of leukemia called multiple myeloma, a cancer of the plasma cells. She also had lesions on her spine and skull. For unknown reasons, myeloma is one of the top ten leading causes of cancer death among African Americans. Tamela is black.

Her first reaction: "I'm going to die," and she thought of her husband, her five-year-old daughter, and her newborn girl. Dr. Redfern said yes, people die every day from this form of cancer, but he said in her case he was "hopeful."

Tamela immediately started treatment. She first had to shrink the tumor with a toxic mix of thalidomide and dexamethasone pills. This was before they even began to fight the cancer itself. Every morning, in the shower, she would pray for healing. That's what she was doing, six weeks later, when her soapy hand brushed her sternum and noticed the lump was gone. She immediately set up another appointment with Dr. Redfern.

At Dr. Redfern's office, Tamela was grinning ear to ear, holding the baby, eager to get back to breast-feeding and restart her catering business. Her mother and Major sat by her side.

"I'm healed, doctor!" Tamela said. "Just like I prayed for. I'm healed—"

Dr. Redfern acknowledged the small bump on her sternum appeared to be only bone. The tests he had ordered showed no sign of cancer in Tamela's body. His next words broke her heart.

"Perhaps," he said. "But this is an aggressive type of cancer, and it could come back. You must go through the entire treatment."

....

After Jesus finished His last supper with His disciples, He wrapped a towel around His waist. Kneeling with a bowl of water in front of them, He began washing their feet and wiping them with the towel He was wrapped with.

When He came to Peter, Peter resisted. Jesus insisted—He wanted Peter not only to allow Jesus to wash his feet, but, more importantly, to learn the lesson the foot washing was intended to teach. After He was finished, He asked them if they understood what He had done.

"If I then, your Lord and Teacher, have washed your feet, you also ought to wash one another's feet. For I have given you an example, that you should do as I have done to you" (John 13:14–15).

Jesus gave His disciples—and each of us—a model for our lives. We need to humbly serve one another. To serve someone means to provide something further. We can only provide or give from what we have been given from God—and one of the most precious gifts we have received is God's comfort in times of pain.

....

For one year, Tamela, her body, and her family went through hell.

Narrow tubes protruded out of her chest from a permanent "port" placed under her skin, which enabled medical personnel to give her chemo and remove blood without injecting her with a needle. She suffered a serious infection when her body rejected the port. Her daughter and her husband shaved her head many times to get ahead of the chemo look.

Tamela, a highly energetic woman, felt nauseous most of the time, and very tired. She had to take high doses of pain medication. Known for her independence, she had to humble herself and allow people to take care of her. She couldn't drive. Major had to take off valuable time from work to help, but he couldn't be around all the time. They scrambled to find someone to stay with the baby and the five-year-old while Tamela went to daily appointments. They needed someone to help prepare meals, tutor their daughter, clean the house, grocery shop, and fill prescriptions.

She had to go into the hospital to receive more chemo. One day she was sick, throwing up; another day she was weak; the next she couldn't get out of bed.

In preparation for her two bone-marrow transplants, Major had to give Tamela two shots per day, each bringing her to tears. The transplants would take fourteen to twenty-one days, and they had to occur within six months of each other.

What made things worse is that she believed she was healed. There was no sign of cancer anywhere in her body.

"God," she asked, "tell me how I can get through this. I have kids. I don't want to die. Please, God, tell me what to do. I need to hear You speak to me. What do I do?"

She knew prayer changes things. So she began to pray. At first it felt like a one-sided conversation. The more Tamela suffered, the more she cried out to God, and the closer to Him she became.

"I realized after days and days of crying out to God that I had a choice to make. I could slip into despair and let it take over, or I could listen to what the Creator of the world had to say about my specific situation. Even if this is my time to die, I praise You," she said.

One of the most powerful ways He comforted her, she said, was through Scripture. She carried Bible verses on note cards with her everywhere, studying them like she studied during her MBA program. She has since designed and printed the note cards, now called "Recipes of Healing," and is sharing them with other cancer patients.

God was bringing her through the most painful experience of her life, and then it clicked. That was her lesson. God was revealing to her what people go through when they have cancer.

HELP
Wanted

In the United States, an estimated 10,701,000 people suffer from some sort of cancer, according to the American Cancer Society.[14]

Immediately Tamela began thinking about "washing the feet" of other cancer patients. Instead of starting her soul-food business again, she decided to apply her organizational skills to start a ministry to serve cancer patients. As soon as she began regaining her strength, she put the wheels in motion to start the ministry.

The apostle Paul tells us in 2 Corinthians 1:3–4, "Blessed be the God and Father of our Lord Jesus Christ, the Father of mercies and God of all comfort, who comforts us in all our tribulation."

We can only give what we have been given.

If you are at a loss about what you can do for someone, start with identifying how God has comforted you. Then pay it forward. You have the power to do that.

Once you can identify His ongoing work in your life, ask God to bring someone who is experiencing the same problem or struggling with the same sin and can benefit from what you have learned.

Now you have a ministry.

Tamela's cancer ministry at the Rock Church presently matches up volunteers with patients from local hospitals to provide child care, cook meals for their families, pick up their medicine, drive them to therapy, clean their homes, provide tutoring for their kids, and run errands.

Whose feet are you washing?

ACTIVITIES

Find someone who is going through a trial you have been through. There may be someone in your life who just lost their job. Has God ever brought you through that? Someone is grieving a death in their family. You may have been through that. If God brought you through divorce, certainly there is someone to whom you are now equipped to minister. You might even be able to prevent a divorce. The possibilities are endless.

Dear God, thank You for bringing me through the trials of my life. Thank You for Your merciful comfort in my life. I pray that You show me how I can pay it forward, washing the feet of someone in my life who is in need. Bring someone to me whom I can comfort with the comfort You have given me.

HEROES

See Tamela at www.milesmcpherson.com.

Ph.DO

Start your own cancer care ministry. Find out how at www.dosomethingworld.org.

24

Theresa

Helping Others Help Others

Therefore I say to you, her sins, which are many, are forgiven, for she loved much. But to whom little is forgiven, the same loves little.

—Luke 7:47

"Theresa, what are you doing to yourself?"

Theresa nearly dropped the phone when she heard her father's voice. She was alone in a hotel room in Los Angeles and had been expecting a call from her next "client." *Not* her dad.

They hadn't talked in years, and she had hit bottom. She was utterly lonely, fed up with her call-girl lifestyle, and yearning to be free.

When Theresa started dancing in clubs at twenty-two, she just wanted to make some quick money. She was a single mom and needed to pay for child care. She started out just stripping, but that led to escorting. The motivation at every stage wasn't the sex or the attention or the power or the drugs and alcohol—though all those things helped to hold her. It was the money: the Corvette, the designer clothes, the private school for her son. She was making up to $30,000 per month in private sessions as a Vegas call girl, and that was hard to walk away from.

She had given her life to Jesus Christ at twenty-one. But that faith decision wasn't yet complete, and it hadn't stopped her from working in the sex industry. Yet, she knew that while her bank account was full, her heart was empty.

Now, sitting on the hotel bed, her dad was on the phone, extending a loving opportunity to get out. With her father's encouragement, Theresa escaped the sex industry and began a new life.

A few months later she caught a story on CNN about a former adult entertainer who had started a ministry to reach other women in the "world's oldest profession." Theresa felt like she had been hit with a lightning bolt. "I knew right then that that was my calling," she said.

She started the San Diego chapter of JC's Girls through the Rock Church, and her volunteers go into strip clubs to build relationships with the women there, making sure each of them knows that not only does God love them, He also provides a way out for them. Just about every stripper in San Diego County has received a pink Bible from the JC's Girls.

For Theresa, though, there is more to it. She is offering the women what she received—a chance to turn their experience into a ministry to others.

....

Sitting on one of the boulders that outlined the well, Jesus watched as a worn-looking Samaritan woman with a pot walked toward Him (John 4).

Historical strife between Jews and Samaritans and the limits religious tradition placed on a rabbi's public contact with women made a conversation between the two of them highly unlikely. Or so the woman thought.

As she lowered her container into the well, Jesus asked for a drink. Surprised, she said (I am paraphrasing), "You're asking me for water? You know my people don't talk to your people."

Without acknowledging the cultural drama, Jesus responded, "How about I give you living water?"

Looking down the deep well and back to the "potless" Jesus, the woman asked, "How are you going to get that kind of water out of there?"

Pointing toward His heart, Jesus replied, "The living water I am talking about, my sister, will come from within."

She wanted such water.

"Before we drink," Jesus answered, pointing toward the woman's city, "go back and get your husband."

She looked at the ground. "I have no husband."

Jesus said, "I know, but you have had five in the past."

The woman knew immediately that Jesus was some kind of prophet. Setting her pot on the ground, she ran back to town and told the men of the city about her encounter with this strange man. Many in the town came to Jesus and believed in Him. Those who believed brought Jesus back to their city, and even more people believed in Him.

• •

"I was scared to death."

Mindy, a friend of Theresa's, looked at the four teenage foster girls she had come to talk to. They were slouched in the two old couches.

"All the dancers had, you know, the perfect bodies . . . ," said Mindy, a petite twenty-four-year-old brunette, as she leaned against the group home's big-screen television in ragged jeans and a baseball T-shirt. "My chest is, you know, all natural, and I was worried I wouldn't make any money, which would mean I was not pretty enough. One of the girls said if I got $50 that first night, that was good. I walked out with $500."

Mindy paused and glanced at the two fifteen-year-olds on the sofa, who looked tense. One was biting her lip. Then she looked at the two seventeen-year-olds, who already were prostitutes. One was bouncing her fake leopard four-inch heels. The other was twisting a strand of bleached hair and staring at the ceiling.

"I felt sexy and powerful—for the first six months."

Mindy and two other women had come to the foster home to talk to the teens about the reality of the adult entertainment industry. After coming out of the Navy and in need of money, Mindy spent three hard years stripping in a club.

"Then a guy got a little too aggressive, and when I didn't want to do what he wanted, he said, 'You ain't nothing but a [#@&!] whore!' That's when I started to realize I needed to get out."

Veronica and Sheila stood up before the two older teens could think of an excuse to leave.

Veronica and Sheila were mother and daughter. Veronica, forty-four years old, had been a prostitute, call girl, escort, and madam for almost thirty years.

"I was on the street at twelve and started working at sixteen. I dove headfirst into working, drugs, and alcohol. I met my pimp when I was eighteen and worked for him seven years. I opened up a brothel in Alaska when I was nineteen. I had two of his kids," Veronica looked over at Sheila and smiled.

HELP *Wanted*

The National Task Force on Prostitution suggests that more than 1 million people in the United States have worked as prostitutes— about 1 percent of American women.[15]

"But because he wasn't really my man, I needed real love, and I began getting it from another guy. When my pimp found out, he beat me with fireplace tools. The only thing that saved me was jumping through a glass door. I was covered in blood. There were two guys who happened to be outside working on their car, and I asked them to call 911. I collapsed."

She survived and went on to work in the business for another twenty years.

It was Sheila's turn. "I was kinda born into the business. I started when I was a teenager too. I didn't think I could pay for college, and my mom was sick, so . . ."

Sheila told the girls that she worked in the escort business for five years. Ironically, her pimp was a childhood friend she had met when they were both ten years old, and who had told her not to get into the business.

Mindy, Veronica, and Sheila all saw themselves in the four foster girls listening to them. They saw where they once had been, and they felt the broken hearts they did not want those young girls to have. Talking with the teenagers was a chance for the former adult entertainment workers to turn their hell into help.

They were there because of Theresa's ministry.

Ministry is not necessarily a formal organization but a response to your own encounter with God: His gracious response to your brokenness; your five husbands; your drug addiction; your lying, cheating, and stealing.

If you really pay attention to how God has interacted with your brokenness and can share that experience, connecting it to someone else's brokenness, you have a ministry.

If you can help them connect their encounter with God to someone else's brokenness, you have given them a ministry.

Each of these women was in that foster home because of Theresa's ministry. Whose ministry are you helping to get started?

ACTIVITIES

Jesus told us to go make disciples, teaching faithful men and women the things we have heard so they can go tell others (Matt. 28:18–20; 2 Tim. 2:2). You can start by inviting a friend to a ministry activity you're involved in. You could try to identify the ministry focus by asking them what type of help they have received from God. This would be a subject they could speak about firsthand. Identify one person whom you could help discover a ministry and place the name in the spaces below.

Dear Lord, please provide the perfect ministry opportunity for _____. Give me the wisdom to help them identify who You want them to encourage. Please prepare their heart to be receptive for this opportunity and use it to nurture in them a heart of service. Lord, please also prepare the people _____ would offer help to.

HEROES

Meet Theresa and the JC's Girls ministry at www.milesmcpherson.com.

Ph.DO

To start a ministry to the strip clubs in your city, go to www.dosomethingworld.org.

25

Noemi

Extraordinary Measures

This kind can come out by nothing but prayer and fasting.

—Mark 9:29

Noemi pushed the VHS tape into the VCR and settled back on the sofa next to her little brother, Marcus. Two of her friends from college, and the friends' parents, were visiting, and they had been looking forward to watching her favorite movie, *Raiders of the Lost Ark*. Marcus turned down the lights and reached for the bowl of popcorn.

The television came to life. But instead of Indiana Jones running across the screen, three completely naked people appeared, having sex. Everyone in the room froze as Noemi lunged to push Eject.

Dad! How could you!

Noemi shriveled in embarrassment. She heard Marcus crack a nervous joke. The others covered their shock with funny comments. She just wanted to crawl into a hole and die.

Noemi had developed early in her adolescence. All through junior and senior high school she had been teased and harassed for her voluptuous body. On top of that, her relationship with her father, Richard, had been distant all those years. She did not feel valued by him, and not once did he ever talk with her about how a man should treat a woman.

What made matters worse was that Richard was a minister. Being disrespected at school is one thing. But if her own dad, a pastor, didn't pay attention to her, she was convinced something must be wrong with *her*.

She turned against herself. When she was seventeen, Noemi gained a hundred pounds in one year. Five foot five, she would spend two decades weighing nearly three hundred pounds.

Then the rift between her and her dad got even wider when she discovered his deep dark secret.

Four years before the VHS peep show, Noemi caught her dad buying porn through the cable TV provider. At that moment it became clear to her that all along her father had loved his addiction to pornography more than his daughter. This made her self-hate even worse.

When she confronted him, he denied the problem. That's also what happened after the VHS fiasco. Marcus and his older brother challenged their father. More denials, and a return to "normal."

Normal? Richard's secret life had destroyed his relationship with his little girl, not to mention undermined his son's respect for him. It had caused him to deceive his wife. And it lost him his pastorate, although he hid the true reason.

Now in her late thirties, Noemi was living with her parents while in between jobs, even though she had not hugged her father or said *I love you* to him in almost twenty years.

One night she felt burdened to check on him. She had an uneasy feeling she might find him deathly ill, or even dead.

No. Her father had snuck onto her own computer to download offensive images. Noemi was so disgusted with him that she had vowed no communication until he got help and apologized to her. She moved out again, and they did not speak for more than a year and a half.

Noemi felt trapped and needed a decisive breakthrough in her life. She knew she could not do it alone. She needed the power of

God. Noemi decided to go on a forty-day fast, consuming only juices and broth.

At the start she prayed, "Lord, help me with Dad. Show me what to do."

....

Surrounded by finger-pointing religious leaders, the disciples were busted.

Rolling around on the ground in the middle of the drama-filled crowd was a demon-possessed boy the disciples were unable to deliver.

The religious leaders had the proof they needed. Jesus and His disciples were a fraud. If Jesus really had the power of God, why couldn't His disciples heal the boy? They were no different than any other false religious leader.

All at once, the crowd turned to greet Jesus as He walked into their midst. Jesus asked the religious leaders what was going on. Before they could answer, the father of the boy complained that His disciples were unable to help his demon-possessed son. Frustrated, Jesus asked the boy's father to bring his son to Him.

Jesus looked at the disciples, the religious leaders, and the father of the boy. He asked them a simple question.

"How long has this been happening to him?" (Mark 9:21).

The distraught man answered, "From childhood. And often [the demon] has thrown him both into the fire and into the water to destroy him. But if You can do anything, have compassion on us and help us" (Mark 9:21–22).

The crowd grew in anticipation that Jesus was getting ready to do something miraculous. They were right.

He healed the boy with these words: "Deaf and dumb spirit, I command you, come out of him and enter him no more!" (Mark 9:25).

The disciples had spent who knows how long praying, throwing water on the boy, dancing around him, waving their hands—all that stuff. But they lacked the power necessary to deliver the boy.

Jesus only had to speak one sentence. Why?

When the disciples got Jesus alone in the house, they asked Him, "Why couldn't we cast out the demon?"

Jesus said, "This kind can come out only through prayer and fasting."

··

There are times in our lives, special circumstances, in which we need more of God's power than other times. The incident with the boy and Jesus illustrates that spiritual power comes with personal surrender.

One ultimate surrender is to deny yourself of the very thing that keeps you alive: food. In addition, the length of your surrender will also have an impact on the amount of power you receive. The Bible says that when you are weak, you are strong, because our weakness fosters a deeper dependence on God.

Moses, Elijah, and Jesus Himself fasted for forty days before intense spiritual assignments.

The longer you deny yourself, the weaker you make yourself—and the more power you may receive. The longer your self-denial, the longer God has to shape and mold your heart.

Noemi wanted to deal with the baggage in her life—through the power of God. She decided to participate in a forty-day period of prayer and fasting that the Rock was holding.

(I am not saying that everyone should conduct a forty-day fast—or a fast of any specific number of days—as if it would be a magic formula. If you do decide to fast, it would be wise to do so under the supervision of a physician. But the longer you can separate and submit yourself solely to God, the more deeply He can shape your heart. If you want God to do big things *through* you, He first needs to do a big thing *in* you. That can best begin to happen by setting aside things on which we are humanly dependent.)

Think about what Noemi was trying to overcome. Thirty-nine years of a dysfunctional relationship. A terrible self-image. Her dad strangled by decades of

HELP
Wanted

Almost half (47 percent) of American families say pornography is a problem in their home.[16]

watching pornography. The power needed to defeat a sexual addiction and mend a broken daddy-daughter relationship was not going to come with a five-minute bedtime prayer. The situation Noemi found herself in would require her to fight a long and intense spiritual battle.

....

Not knowing what to expect God to do, Noemi faithfully followed her regime. Thirty days into her fast, she had lost thirty-five pounds. But she was still waiting for evidence of God's power to impact her inner self and her relationship with her dad.

Then something happened. Noemi is a high school teacher who cares deeply about her students. One day she found herself serving as a sort of referee in a family dispute between a sixteen-year-old and the girl's parents. As Noemi watched them scream at each other, she saw that the mom did not know how to apologize and that the teenager did not know how to forgive her mother.

God opened her eyes and she saw her dad, a man who did not know how to say he was sorry. She saw herself as the daughter who needed to forgive. She called her father, and within an hour, he was at her door.

"Dad, I want you to know I do not need to hear you say you're sorry. I forgive you for everything you did to me and everything that happened. I love you."

At that, Richard dropped his head into his hands and sobbed. Through his weeping he said, "Thank you. Thank you. I have been praying to God to show me a sign that He is still hearing me. I am sorry, Noemi. I don't know the damage I have caused, but I know I caused it."

Through his tears of repentance Richard kept saying, *I have my daughter back*. For the next ninety minutes they hugged, cried, and said *I love you* more than they had their entire lives.

Prayer is an act of surrender. It means depending on a God that you believe is superior to you. The deeper and more regular your prayer is, the more of God's power you will secure. "The effective, fervent prayer of a righteous man avails much" (James 5:16).

The power that Noemi received in her forty-day fast not only freed her up physically but spiritually as well.

Noemi was shackled not only by her weight but by a negative perception about who she is. She is on her way to a weight of 145 pounds and is training to run a marathon. "I'm not who I was. I'm free," she says.

She can now hug and kiss her dad, and he is open about his problem.

God wants to bring about a spiritual breakthrough in your life too. He has a powerful work He wants to do in your heart.

Surrender yourself to Him today. It does not necessarily need to be during forty days of fasting. Ask Him how. He will guide you.

ACTIVITIES

Identify one major problem in your life that could benefit from an extra dose of the power of God. It could be a financial need, a relational concern, a health issue, or a career decision. No matter what it is, there is a spiritual component. Commit a specific period of time to fast and pray for the power to overcome that which holds you back from being what God has called you to be.

Dear God, please give me the courage to surrender myself to You beyond what is comfortable. Please guide me to the exact sacrifice You want me to make and the length of time You want me to make it. Lord, when I do this, please give me clear evidence of Your power, that I may know You have heard my prayer.

Take an extra step and "porn-proof" your computer. Go to www.dosomethingworld.org to learn how.

For prayer and fasting tools, go to www.milesmcpherson.com. Note that full or partial fasting for an extended period of time should be done under the supervision of a medical professional.

DO Something! Myth 5

*I need to be superman/superwoman
if I am doing something
through God's power.*

The Lies Behind It

- God's power is always displayed in visible, measurable ways.
- Everyone must be immediately "fixed" or "helped." Your burden is to do it all.
- Being the best or the greatest is what God gives you His power for.

The Truth

- Even though God's power is displayed in ways we can see, there are times when its greatest work is done in the hearts of people.
- We will never, in this life, see all that God does.

Scripture

Who then is Paul, and who is Apollos, but ministers through whom you believed, as the Lord gave to each one? I planted, Apollos watered, but God gave the increase.

—1 Corinthians 3:5–6

Something to Remember

We are called to do *some*thing, but not *EVERY*thing. In the end, God is the one who brings about change in His way and His timing. Our responsibility is to simply play our position on the team and obey by faith.

Part 6

Passion

Never Give Up

During the last week of Jesus' life, Passion Week, He was physically, emotionally, mentally, and even spiritually tormented more than during His entire life. Yet His **passion** would not let Him give up on His mission. He was betrayed by one of His disciples, denied by another, and falsely accused by religious leaders. He even felt forsaken by His own Father. But He never quit.

> Jesus said to him, "No one, having put his hand to the plow, and looking back, is fit for the kingdom of God."
>
> — Luke 9:62

26

Cody

Preparation—Trusting Your Training

Now when they bring you to the synagogues and magistrates and authorities, do not worry about how or what you should answer, or what you should say. For the Holy Spirit will teach you in that very hour what you ought to say.

— Luke 12:11–12

"That is the wrong street! Get out right now! It is a trap!"

The urgent voice crackled over the handheld radio to the men in the Mercedes.

Cody slammed on the brakes, throwing his four passengers forward.

The guy riding shotgun cursed. "Cody! What's going on?"

He and his fellow Navy SEAL teammates, in civilian clothes, had followed the lead vehicle into a roundabout. They were part of a caravan conducting an ISR (Initial Surveillance and Reconnaissance) in Mosul, a dimly lit city in northern Iraq. Their mission: check out intelligence on hot spots of the enemy and determine whether their small attack teams should engage or call in a larger unit. Three

Humvees providing emergency combat and medical support were in the rear. Guided by GPS, the lead vehicle had taken the second right turn off the roundabout. Cody had swung down the first one, heading right into the trap.

Their Mercedes' headlights lit up a primitive roadblock of cinderblocks propped on their sides, lined up across the street from side to side.

Cody looked in the rearview mirror. Their black car with tinted windows was alone.

That's when the radio crackled.

Cody quickly realized he had just seconds to make a decision. Something was moving in the dark dead end. They were sitting ducks.

Shadows beyond the cinderblocks began running barricades on either side of the road.

Pop! Snap! Pop! Snap! Bursts of light from the enemy's AK-47s pierced the dim light as the bullets broke the sound barrier and flew past them.

The navigator in the backseat yelled, "Get out of here!"

Ducking below the steering wheel, Cody slammed the gear into reverse and stomped on the accelerator, keeping his eyes on the side mirror.

The lives of the men were not entirely in the hands of Cody's training.

• •

Dozens of shouting scribes, elders, and priests in tassel-covered, embroidered robes and tall, Shriner-like hats stuffed themselves into the high priest's chambers. They shouted and shoved each other to get close enough to hit Jesus, who silently stood still. Drops of blood covered His forehead as He stood in front of dozens of enraged religious leaders.

For the entire three years of His ministry, the Jewish leaders had been trying to discredit Jesus. Whenever they tried to catch Him in a lie, He ended up making them look stupid. Now it was the middle of the night, and they had Jesus on their home turf. He appeared to have no leverage, and the religious leaders began drilling Him with questions, waiting and listening for any hint of an "I AM God" claim.

If Jesus said anything close to claiming to be God's Son, they would absolutely "go postal" on Him.

174

The high priest waved his hand to quiet the crowd. This was the moment they were waiting for. He got in Jesus' face and asked one very simple and direct question: "Are You the Christ, the Son of the Blessed?"

Jesus looked around the room at the hate in the eyes of His critics, and then back at the high priest. "I am. And you will see the Son of Man sitting at the right hand of the Power, and coming with the clouds of heaven" (Mark 14:61–62).

Oh yeah, they "went postal" all right, and FedEx and UPS and Unabomber and . . .

Let me tell you why.

His response was a twofold offense to the religious leaders. First, He identified Himself with the God who spoke to Moses from the burning bush by identifying Himself as "I AM."

Second, He claimed to be the one whom the Old Testament predicted would judge the world and sit in a seat of eternal judgment (Dan. 7:13). Jesus was telling them, "You may be judging Me now in this earthly court, but I will be your eternal judge."

No! He did not just say that! they thought.

HELP
Wanted

Nearly one in five, or about 300,000, soldiers who have served in Iraq or Afghanistan has post-traumatic stress disorder or major depression.[17]

· ·

"Go! Go! Go!"

Pop! Pop! Pop! Snap! Snap! Bullets flew by the car and sparked off of the street. Cody's mind was racing. Strategizing. This was no time for winging it. Failure meant death—for four men plus himself.

As part of his preparation to be a Navy SEAL, Cody had spent months in Basic Underwater Demolition/SEAL (BUD/S), training daily in guerilla warfare, firearms, and survival skills. Thank God emergency driving was part of that advanced training.

During drills, instructors had ambushed Cody's team with simulated gunfire, grenade launchers, tear gas, and artillery simulators. The goal was to create as much chaos as possible to force the would-be SEALs to focus only on the information necessary to accomplish the mission.

Cody focused.

The Mercedes was carrying thousands of rounds of machine gun ammunition, grenade launchers, medical supplies, navigation equipment, and communication systems, in addition to the five men. Cody knew it was too overloaded for its diesel engine capacity to maneuver quickly.

Gotta turn this rig around without flipping it over and making my guys sitting ducks—

If he tried to spin the car too quickly, it would easily flip. When a car is in reverse, the weight is pushed to the front tires, which (if the car is turned too quickly) can roll it onto its side.

Cody needed to back out of the street as fast as he could, then redistribute the weight of the vehicle away from the front of the car and spin the steering wheel 180 degrees while pressing on the clutch and shifting into first gear. And he needed to do it *now*.

Pop! Snap! The bullets were flying.

In one movement, Cody pressed in the clutch, transferred the weight toward the back tires, spun the steering wheel, and swung the car around. He shifted, let out the clutch, and gunned the Mercedes out of the street and around the corner. Out of the line of fire.

"Yes! You da man, son!" Everyone in the car was screaming. "That's right, boy! They can't get us now!"

The radio snapped on. "Is everybody okay? Anybody hit, commander?" came a gruff voice.

"We're okay," Cody said, dazed.

"Well, apparently they trained you well back home. Now get your butts back to the caravan!"

Cody's trainers knew that he would face an emergency and that he needed to be prepared—for his sake and for the sake of those he was responsible for.

Your emergency is coming too. What training will you rely on when it comes? Will you trust God? Or will you start cursing? Yelling? Screaming? Worrying yourself to death?

What manual has prepared you for your life's emergency? God's Word has laid out for you and me, in advance, the guidelines for how to deal with the toughest situations. God is always prepared, and our circumstances never catch Him off guard.

It will be your natural tendency to go with your gut. But making a spur-of-the-moment reaction is often what gets us in trouble. Impulse reactions are useful if they are based on proper God-preparation. "The preparations of the heart belong to man, but the answer of the tongue is from the LORD" (Prov. 16:1).

It is our responsibility to get and stay prepared—to study the Bible, God's manual for life, and to pray and worship regularly. But not only that. We must be ready to rely on that preparation, allowing God to direct us through that crisis moment. God has provided for us the tools necessary to prepare us to deal with our tough times, not naturally but supernaturally.

Passion will rely only on the preparations of God. If you are going to *do something* of eternal value when that moment comes, it will be because you passionately trusted your preparation made by God in your life.

ACTIVITIES

Identify one area of weakness in your character that will most likely lead to disobedience when times get tough. This would be the area in your life that needs to be better prepared for the unexpected drama that is sure to come. Perhaps it is your temper (Ps. 4:4); anxiety (Phil. 4:6–8); pride (Prov. 29:23); impatience (Ps. 46:10); lack of self-control (Prov. 3:5–6); anger (Prov. 15:1); not taking advice (Prov. 15:22); being too quick to speak (Prov. 18:13); worrying (Matt. 6:31–33); using bad language (Eph. 4:29). Memorize the appropriate verse as a tool to help you get it right when everything around you is falling apart.

Dear God, give me the passion to do what it takes to prepare me for whatever emergency is coming. Prepare my heart to learn and trust in Your Word, especially during that crisis moment that will undoubtedly catch me off guard. Give me the discipline to not only prepare until I get it right, but to practice until I can't get it wrong.

27

Major Carl

Purpose—Loving the Difficult

Father, forgive them for they do not know what they do.

—Luke 23:34

Felix strutted down West 47th Street in Manhattan, sporting his brand-new Timberlands and Sean Jean jeans on his way to work at the Salvation Army's Theatre 315. It was actually the Salvation Army church building, built as an outreach to the theater community. Every so often they hosted special community events. As a stagehand, Felix hung lights, built and took apart sets, organized the seats, and did whatever else needed to be done.

Felix was a 5-foot-6 Hispanic guy with a happy smile and a warm, lover-boy personality. "What's up, Felix?" someone called when he walked into the building. "Hey Felix," another stagehand yelled out.

Major Carl, Felix's boss and pastor of the 120-seat church, had met him at the adult rehabilitation center (ARC) three years ago. Felix was recovering from alcohol and cocaine addictions. As one of the chaplains of the ARC, Major Carl held Bible studies for those in rehab, which often led to an ongoing relationship with many of the members in the program.

Major Carl has seen the good, the bad, and the ugly in Felix, but today Felix was putting in a hard day's work and would earn $250.

As Major Carl walked through the lobby, Felix ran up behind him, placed his arm on his shoulder, and during a long hug said, "I want to thank you for all you've done for me, brutha."

"You're welcome, man," Carl said, leaning back to check Felix out full-on.

Felix looked up with a Christmas morning smile and said, "Hey, listen, I know payday is next week, but can I get an advance? I need to get a metro card for the train and food for my four kids."

Major Carl thought, *Didn't he just buy a weekly metro card two days ago? Did he sell it? Trade it for drugs? Who knows?*

He gave Felix the money anyway. After all, it was an advance on money he had earned.

Several months later Felix's "baby's mama," Lucille, showed up at the church on Felix's payday. She came with her current boyfriend, Felix's four kids, and a "feel-sorry-for-me-or-there-will-be-drama" look on her face.

Lucille was there to get manipulation money from Felix. Carl had given Felix four wrapped toys to give to the kids, so while the "blackmail" was in progress, he asked them how they had liked the Christmas gifts he had given them. He got nothing but blank stares. Something happened between the church and the Christmas tree.

Felix claimed their "crackhead" mother sold them. Lucille claimed Felix never brought them home. Carl made a mental note to always give the gifts to the kids himself from then on.

Not long after that, Felix called Carl asking for a place to stay. He had just been evicted from his apartment. Ironically, the call came only two days after Felix walked out of the theatre with more than enough in his paycheck for rent money. He spent those two days smoking his rent through a crack pipe.

Major Carl let him stay in the Salvation Army residential facility until he could get back on his feet.

Reaching His bread-filled hand into the bowl, Jesus looked into the eyes of a disciple who, in three seconds, He would give the bread to and say, "What you do, do quickly" (John 13:27).

But what a long three seconds it would be.

As Judas sat at the table with his fellow disciples, his guilt wouldn't allow him to look at Jesus too long.

With his eyes shifting back and forth, he was being convicted by the Lord's love. In those three seconds, Jesus had flashbacks of their relationship.

For three years I taught you about the kingdom of God. You watched Me exercise power over disease, demons, and death.

You know how much I agonized over the hurting people I ministered to. We just had our last supper together, where I explained the pain I will go through when I am turned over to the religious leaders who will torture and kill me.

I just finished washing your feet, teaching you to be a servant. I placed you in the seat of honor, right next to me, so I can share this meal with you, in hopes of loving you out of your evil.

Jesus loved Judas the entire three years they were together, knowing he would betray Him. Now they were sitting face-to-face, with the devil instigating Judas's famous betrayal.

The three seconds were now over. Jesus said, "Go ahead, do what you need to do."

....

"Major Carl, Felix is on the phone," his secretary said.

Walking to the phone, he thought, *What has he gotten himself into now?*

Major Carl never felt confident that Felix would follow through with his promises or would spend his money on what he said that he needed it for. In fact, Carl knew he didn't know the full extent of the trouble Felix was constantly in. So why continue to help him? Why had Carl spent seven years on a guy like Felix, who had again and again shown that he was on a mission to destroy his own life?

"Major Carl, I'm in jail. I need help."

Felix had gone along with a scheme Lucille and her boyfriend had dreamed up. The boyfriend would play the pimp and lure guys into the apartment to get some "action" with Lucille. Once inside, Felix and the boyfriend would beat up the "john," steal his money, and kick him out of the apartment.

All three were arrested for assault and battery. Felix's four kids, who were in the bedroom at the time this was going on, were now in foster care.

Sitting in jail with no one to go to, Felix was given one phone call. Major Carl was his first thought.

There was only one person in his life who had been there for him through thick and thin. Major Carl.

Sometimes God will entrust you with a "problem child" to love. Someone who will require more attention than most. A person who will test the extent of your passion to love those who will do nothing but take advantage of you.

When Jesus told His disciples that one of them would betray Him, He also said that the betrayal was predicted and necessary. But that in no way justified Judas's actions. Jesus was saying, "Evil will come, but don't be that guy through whom it comes."

Just as easily as we can be hurt by someone, God can use that hurt to nurture deep spiritual health in our lives. Passion will keep us true to our purpose of following Jesus, even in the face of our enemies.

Though your enemies surround you, if God is for you, it does not matter what they do against you or to you. They cannot hinder God's purposes in your life, as long as you remain obedient.

Is there someone in your life who is hard to love? Someone who seems to be determined to irritate, disrespect, or upset you?

Felix is out of jail now but on the run. The police are after him for something else. Major Carl expects a call any day.

HELP
Wanted

More than 10.5 million children in the United States are living with one or more substance-abusing parents.[18]

Major Carl still visits Felix's kids to pray for and encourage them with the hopes that when they are in need they will remember, it was a man of God who helped them and their dad. Maybe they will call one of God's faithful when they have nowhere else to go.

ACTIVITIES

Complete this sentence: It is hard for me to be nice and love _____ because they make me feel _____.

Replace your hard heart with love by expressing God's love toward them. As long as it is safe, consider sending them a card or calling them and apologizing for the condition of your relationship, or just giving them one simple compliment.

Dear Lord, please fill me with the passion to fulfill my purpose of loving my enemies. Lord, please open my eyes to realize that withholding Your love from them would be a disobedient thing for me to do. Empower me today to express Your love to them in a very convincing and unmistakable way.

HEROES

Meet Major Carl at www.milesmcpherson.com.

Ph.DO

To volunteer with your local Salvation Army, go to www.salvationarmy.org.

28

Mark

Pain—Walking into It

And He said, "Abba, Father, all things are possible for You. Take this cup away from Me; nevertheless, not what I will, but what You will."

—Mark 14:36

Mark bounced up and down as his fire truck rushed through the Brooklyn Battery Tunnel into downtown Manhattan. He already could see huge black clouds of smoke spiraling up from the World Trade Center. It was September 11, 2001.

The F.D.N.Y. firefighter flipped open his cell phone and called his wife, Lisa. She was in their living room, busy homeschooling their five children. "Honey? It looks really bad . . ." He asked her to pray. "I love you," he said. The signal faded.

The entire world was watching after terrorists crashed two jets into the trade center's two quarter-mile-high financial buildings, 110 stories high. The congestion in the street was like rush hour on steroids. People were running in every direction, dodging burning debris raining down. The air was gray with ash.

Between the burning North Tower and South Tower sat the 22-floor, steel-framed Marriott World Trade Center hotel. It had more than a thousand registered guests that morning. That's where the firefighters of Mark's ladder company headed, running to meet several dozen other firefighters in a makeshift staging area in the lobby. Dozens of hotel guests, staff, and emergency personnel were milling around. Battalion chiefs were frantically strategizing their next move, not knowing the unthinkable was about to happen.

Once inside, Mark noticed that people outside the lobby were running away from the hotel. He rushed to the window, looked up, and saw the South Tower begin to collapse on itself like a giant house of cards. It sounded like claps of thunder as each floor exploded upon the next.

"Run!" he yelled.

The firefighters scattered. Mark and his crew dove into the lounge area of the hotel lobby.

At home, glued to the television, Mark's wife saw the destroyed tower bury the Marriott. She switched the TV off and clutched her heart for a moment. She turned to her children. "We need to pray for Daddy right now."

....

Drops of blood and sweat dripped from Jesus' trembling forehead as the heavy burden of what lay ahead pulled Him to the ground in the Garden of Gethsemane.

"My soul is exceedingly sorrowful, even to death," He said to His disciples. "Stay here and watch" (Mark 14:34). But they wandered off and fell asleep under the stars, and now they were barely visible in the dark under the trees of the garden.

After walking into the garden away from His disciples, Jesus doubled over in anticipation of the pain that He would soon experience. He asked God for an alternative plan to the suffering He was about to go through.

The disciple who watched over the ministry's money would sell Him out for his own financial gain (Mark 14:10–11). One of the three members of His executive committee (Peter) would, on three separate occasions, deny even knowing Him, even with curse words (Matt. 26:69–74). Jesus would be beaten, spat upon, and rejected by the very people He came to save. His beard would be ripped out and His face would be punched and His head scraped by inch-long thorns. His body would be broken with rods, whips, and nails. Worst of all, He would actually be turned into the one thing His Father cannot even look at: sin.

Knowing all of this was moments away, Jesus made one simple request to his Father: "Abba Father, all things are possible for You. Take this cup from Me; nevertheless, not what I will, but what You will" (Mark 14:36).

HELP
Wanted

There are approximately 1,720,000 firefighters, police officers and detectives, and correctional officers in the United States, according to the Bureau of Labor Statistics and the United States Fire Administration.[19]

• •

The impact of the disintegrating Tower 2 slamming into the Marriott forced the security gate in front of the lounge to crash down, forming a cage over the firefighters. The typhoon-force wind from the collapse tossed Mark and his men around like leaves.

Although news reports say an estimated fifty people died in the destruction of the hotel—forty-one of them firefighters—Mark and his men did not. As they stumbled out of the destroyed hotel, they could only see a few feet in front of them because of the swirling dust from the crushed skyscrapers. Breathing was like trying to inhale with your face in a bowl of flour.

Out on West Street, Mark and his men found a *New York Daily News* photographer half under a car, with his leg broken. They picked him up and headed toward an office building across the street. They crammed themselves into one of the street-level shops. The door was locked, but a large window had been blown out.

That's when the North Tower came crashing down. With the deafening rumble of an earthquake, 110 stories pancaked, sending pieces of the skyscraper in a billowing cloud of dust and debris all over downtown Manhattan.

Finding bottled water in the shop, the men washed out their coated eyes and gulped down the cool drink. They rested for a few moments. Then they braved the dust cloud again. Eventually they reached the East River, where they put the injured photojournalist on a boat— Mark can't remember what kind of boat, and he doesn't know what happened to the man. Many of the injured were being taken to the park on Liberty Island, where a triage center had been set up.

Mark ended up being taken to a hospital on Staten Island.

....

Every day, firefighters, police officers, military personnel, people who work in rough neighborhoods, and countless others voluntarily put themselves in harm's way for people they do not know. Sometimes they put themselves at risk on behalf of people who do not appreciate them.

They understand the risks associated with their jobs, but their passion to help others far exceeds the fear of those risks. Just as Jesus physically and emotionally suffered from the anticipation of what lay before him, don't be surprised if you have unpleasant reactions to thinking about what lies ahead of you. A racing heart, sweaty palms, nausea, and sleepless nights do not mean that what you're facing is not part of God's plan.

Jesus voluntarily walked into an uncomfortably painful situation that He preferred to avoid, and you will undoubtedly be called to do the same. If Jesus was successful in getting through His painful situation, so will you be too—as long you obey God.

When you allow your passion to lead you to do something, despite the pain involved, you will be able to look pain in the face and voluntarily walk into it.

The temptation would be to cut corners in your obedience to avoid the suffering. Jesus asked for an alternative to His suffering, so don't be surprised if you want to do the same.

But your desire to please God must ultimately supersede your desire to please yourself and avoid discomfort.

ACTIVITIES

Identify one act of obedience to God that you are putting off because of the perceived difficulty related to obeying Him.

Write down three simple things you need to do in order to complete your obedience.

And the next time you see a firefighter, a police officer, or military personnel, walk over and thank them for putting themselves in harm's way on our behalf.

Dear God, thank You for having the passion to voluntarily walk into the pain of the cross. I realize that You may ask me to do something that might be difficult to do, so please give me the courage to be obedient in the face of pain.

29

Lisa

Power—Doing Nothing

Or do you think that I cannot now pray to My Father, and He will provide Me with more than twelve legions of angels?

—Matthew 26:53

"We're looking for a peaceful resolution for this tragedy without retaliation against the young man who took Marcella's life."

Lisa Ortiz looked nervous but determined. With her brown hair pulled back in a ponytail, she stood in her driveway surrounded by reporters and cameras from all of San Diego County's major news media. She glanced at me. I was there to support her and her husband. Also there were two other pastors, San Diego's police chief, two players from the San Diego Chargers, and four parents who had lost children to gang violence as she had just a week before.

Lisa's twenty-one-year-old daughter, Marcella, had been at a house party when a fight broke out. Marcella had recently graduated from beauty school and was making career plans. She had attended the Rock Church for a year, growing in her commitment to Christ. For about a year, she had asked her mother to come to church with her, but Lisa kept putting her off.

That night, a nineteen-year-old local gang member got in a fight and was kicked out of the party. But he came back, stood in the street, and sprayed the house with bullets. Marcella was hit in the back.

Within hours she was dead.

Within a day, the word in the neighborhood was that the murderer had a price on his head. Rumors of retaliation filled the streets.

I asked Lisa and John if they would participate in a news conference to ask that no one kill their daughter's murderer, and to pray for peace. They said yes, because they didn't want another parent to go through what they were going through.

At the end of the news conference, a reporter asked John the million-dollar question. "Most people would want their child's killer punished. Why are you asking for him to be protected?"

How can you resist the urge for revenge?

....

"Rise, let us be going. See, My betrayer is at hand," Jesus said (Matt. 26:46). He reached down to help His sleepy disciples off the ground.

Orange light, flickering through the trees, lit up the night sky as dozens of soldiers and religious leaders marched up the mountain to arrest Jesus. The disciples, now wide awake, spun in panic as the torches circled behind them. Judas walked up to Jesus and kissed Him. Then he backed away as soldiers tied Jesus up and dragged Him away.

Why didn't Jesus resist? Judas's betrayal was sinister, the torture would be excruciating, the trials would be unfair, and the death humiliating. Why didn't He fight back? Why didn't He use His superman powers to save Himself?

It was clear He did not want to be arrested. Just before Judas arrived, Jesus prayed three times, asking the Father to come up with another way to pay for the sins of the world. Jesus would have preferred to avoid the suffering of the cross, but each time He ended His prayer by saying, "Father, if it is Your will, take this cup away from Me; nevertheless not My will, but Yours, be done" (Luke 22:42).

There is no doubt that Jesus had the power to set Himself free.

189

During Jesus' arrest, Peter grabbed a sword from one of the soldiers and sliced off the ear of the high priest's servant. Pointing to Peter, Jesus told him to put the sword back, warning that we cannot accomplish God's purposes with man's power. ("Not by might nor by power, but by My Spirit," Zech. 4:6.) While the servant held the side of his head and moaned, Jesus picked up the severed flesh, pressed it against the bleeding wound, and *bada-boom bada-bing*, the ear was like new. He could have used that power to melt the servant's head instead of healing his ear.

Instead, His passion to use God's power only for God's purpose restrained Him. He even said, "Or do you think that I cannot now pray to My Father, and He will provide Me with more than twelve legions of angels?" (Matt. 26:53). That meant He had as many as 72,000 angelic soldiers standing at attention in heaven, waiting for the order. The Old Testament tells us that one angel killed 185,000 Assyrian soldiers in one night. Imagine what 72,000 angels could have done.

He could have called on them, but He didn't. When the soldiers arrived on the mountain, Jesus asked, "Who do you seek?" The power of Jesus' response, "I AM He," knocked all the soldiers backward onto the ground. He could have destroyed those men. But He was confident that His time to reign was just around the corner.

Jesus' passion to use His spiritual power to only fulfill God's purpose applied not only to defeating His enemies but to controlling His desire to resist His enemies.

He knew it was time to be arrested and crucified.

He acknowledged to His disciples that this was the time for the power of darkness to do its thing. He said to the religious leaders who came to arrest Him, "This is your hour, and the power of darkness" (Luke 22:53).

He knew He had to stick it out for only one more day and use the power of God to maintain His focus on His goal of paying for the sins of the world.

• •

The first time Lisa walked into the Rock Church's sanctuary, she burst into tears. And it wasn't because she was there to make arrangements for her daughter's funeral.

Here was the place that helped her daughter begin to turn her life around.

This was the church where Marcella wanted to share her God-experience with Lisa.

Now it was too late, and reality was hitting Lisa all at once.

On the day of the funeral, she and I talked in the green room behind the stage before the service. She decided to publicly give her life to Jesus Christ. But she asked me to include a traditional altar call after my sermon. Lisa wanted to get up and walk forward as an example to her family and Marcella's friends. More than thirty people came forward and gave their lives to the Lord.

Because of that change of heart, Lisa and John, even through the pain, could put God's goals ahead of their natural parental desire for revenge.

I was sitting next to Lisa at the gravesite, watching family and friends place flowers on Marcella's casket before it was lowered into the ground.

"John and I have been talking," Lisa said, "and we want to do something to turn this into a positive for the community."

That's when we decided to hold a news conference and plead for the killer's life.

"It would just make me sick if I didn't forgive this guy. You have to look at the big picture and find out what good we can find in this," Lisa said. John echoed the sentiment.

The reporter at the press conference couldn't understand why parents would think anything positive or protective toward their child's killer. Even if they wanted to, how could they find such compassion amidst their pain?

He did not understand that the power of God, in addition to comforting them through their pain, also provided them with the self-control and discipline necessary for a mother and father to forgive their daughter's killer.

HELP *Wanted*

Criminal gangs commit as much as 80 percent of the crime in many communities, according to law enforcement officials throughout the nation.[20]

Passion to make our lives count in the eyes of God will direct His power only toward activities that honor Him. Sometimes it comes in the form of self-control, preventing our feelings from getting in the way of what God wants to accomplish through us.

John and Lisa are passionate about using the power of God to resist the natural inclination for revenge and to pursue God's greatest good out of the situation.

Being obedient in life is about not only doing the right things but also not doing the wrong things. There will often be times in your life when God will tell you to be still and know that He is God (Ps. 46:10). That is, *be still and do something by doing nothing.*

If you are going to do something significant for God, it will require a display of God's supernatural power, not only through you, but also in your own life in the form of self-restraint.

ACTIVITIES

Identify one unproductive, God-dishonoring habit you have, such as cursing, getting angry, overeating, worrying, gossiping, or micromanaging. For one day, prayerfully focus God's power on holding yourself back from doing it. You will be amazed at how much power you have access to. Remember to ask the Invisible Man, the Holy Spirit, for His help.

Dear Lord, please give me the self-control and discipline to focus all of my efforts on that which glorifies You. Please keep me from saying discouraging words, thinking unproductive thoughts, and wasting valuable time doing things that do not honor Your purpose for my life.

HEROES

Hear Lisa's story at www.milesmcpherson.com.

30

Rico

Passion—Finishing Strong

Well done, good and faithful servant; you have been faithful over a few things, I will make you ruler over many things. Enter into the joy of your lord.

—Matthew 25:23

I could hear Rico's parents crying quietly in the backseat. As the officiating pastor, I sat in my dark suit next to the driver as we drove behind Rico's hearse.

We had just finished Rico's funeral at the Rock Church in San Diego. With a thousand people attending, it was one of the largest law enforcement funerals the city had ever seen. The police chief, the mayor, the sheriff, a Marine captain, and an Army general all were there and spoke.

Now we were following Rico's hearse to Fort Rosecrans National Cemetery. At every intersection along the three-mile ride, motorcycle cops blocked the cross traffic. People lined up on both sides of the street, saluting, holding their hands over their hearts, and waving American flags. Even little kids held their hands to their brows.

Fort Rosecrans is a huge military graveyard at the tip of the peninsula that separates the Pacific Ocean from the San Diego Bay. Rows and rows of white tombstones crisscross the grounds. Five hundred law enforcement officers and military personnel from the U.S. Marine Corps, San Diego County Sheriff's Department, San Diego Police Department, and U.S. Army stood at attention at the gravesite.

The casket sat on the pavement in front of a stone table holding medals Rico earned through faithful service. With mechanical precision, a soldier retrieved each medal one by one and handed them to the general standing nearby. He then explained their meaning to the crowd and, kneeling, presented them to Rico's family.

Just before the 21-gun salute, a half dozen soldiers folded the American flag covering Rico's casket and gave it to his nine-year-old daughter.

....

Jesus' head knocked against the cross as it fell back just under the sign that read *King of the Jews*. The blood collecting in his lungs bubbled out of His mouth. Gasping for air, He pushed down on His nailed feet, trying to lift His trembling body so that He could draw a breath. The crowd below taunted Him. "Save yourself!" they shouted. "Come down from the cross . . ." (Mark 15:29–32).

In three words, He gave His last Bible lesson as black clouds swirled above Him (Matt. 27:45).

"It is finished!" He cried.

That was His final sermon, complete with a visual illustration. *What* was finished? His life? Yes. Anything else?

The brief, first-century "Jesus movement" certainly looked finished—as in finished off, over, done, *kaput*. One of His disciples had betrayed Him and then committed suicide (Matt. 27:3–5). Another had denied Him when He needed him the most (Luke 22:54–62). At His trial, the very people He came to save sentenced Him to death and let a known criminal walk free (Luke 23:18–21). The rest of His disciples were running scared (Matt. 26:56), and His critics were mocking Him.

So if everything had fallen apart around Him, and the world was no different than it was when He began His ministry, what exactly was Jesus finished doing?

Jesus had finished fulfilling His role in the Father's plan of salvation.

Taking advantage of all the *preparations* made for Him, He accomplished His *purpose* of obeying God. He converted the *pain* associated with His mission into the spiritual *power* necessary to honor the Father and fuel a *passion* that would not let Him quit.

Because Jesus was faithful to each of these components of God's plan, He was able to say, *It is finished*!

That is our goal too.

During the funeral, many people spoke about Federico "Rico" G. Borjas, and the church ran a beautiful video about his life.

From everything Rico did, it appeared he had pushed himself to tackle always more challenging positions of service.

First he joined the Marine Corps out of high school and made "Iron Man" in boot camp. After the Marines, he joined the San Diego County Sheriff's Department and served as a correctional officer. He later became a San Diego police officer and, after four years, became a Special Weapons and Tactics team (SWAT) officer. He was also the first person in his family to graduate from college, finishing a degree in legal studies. He did all of this as a single dad.

But when his childhood friend died in the Iraq war, Rico felt compelled to serve his country in a more significant way. He joined the U.S. Army Reserves and was deployed as a sergeant to eastern Afghanistan.

Just three weeks after arriving in October 2008, Rico made the ultimate sacrifice. While on patrol, he was killed by an enemy sniper.

As early as the third chapter in the Bible, God required bloodshed for sins to be forgiven. Consequently, throughout the Old Testament, His people sacrificed animals to God as a form of worship and as payment for sins. The sacrifice was not sinless, though; and God's children continued to sin, so the blood sacrifices had to continue.

Jesus' death was also a blood sacrifice and intended to be the sacrifice of all sacrifices. It not only had to be a blood sacrifice but a sinless one. He gave His life as final payment for our sins.

Throughout the Bible, God always gave the giver of the sacrifice some sort of evidence that He had either accepted or rejected the sacrifice.

When Cain and Abel gave their sacrifices to God in Genesis 4, God rejected Cain's because it was not a blood sacrifice. He accepted Abel's, Cain's brother. (Consequently, Cain was angry, and he killed his brother in revenge.)

The sacrifices of Abraham (Gen. 15:9–17) and Manoah (Judg. 13:1–22) were shown to be accepted when God sent fire down to roast the sacrifices.

Noah knew his sacrifice was accepted because God made a covenant with him never to flood the earth again.

In Jesus' case, three things happened that affirmed His sacrifice as acceptable: The graves broke open and the dead were raised (Matt. 27:52)—this was evidence that the power of death was defeated. Also, the veil in the temple was ripped from the top down (Matt. 27:51)—now all people had access to God, not just the high priest. And finally, Jesus was honored in heaven, seated at the right hand of the Father.

The acceptable sacrifice of Jesus' death validated the fact that He was indeed finished.

Only God can determine if a sacrifice is acceptable. God will only respond with "Well done, good and faithful servant" if you have been faithful doing what you *should* have, through every aspect of His plan for your life.

This is not an issue of earning your salvation, as if through good works. Jesus' death paid for sins in full. We only need to accept Him as Savior for salvation. But receiving Christ is only the beginning of God's plan for us. His *entire* three-year ministry played an important role in the salvation of all the countless people who would come after Him.

Your personal mission will be finished when you have executed your aspect of God's plan of salvation.

•••

Following the church service part of the funeral, after the last person emptied the sanctuary, a second pastor and I stood alone in front of the casket. Then down the aisle they came. Eight uniformed military men marched in precise formation to the front of the church to carry Rico out to the hearse. In unison they grabbed the poles on the side of the casket and lifted him up. With tears in his eyes, the leader whispered a command: "Let's take him home."

Rico had finished his faithful service to the Marines, the sheriff's department, the police department, the Army Reserves, college, his parents, and most of all, his daughter.

What about you?

Your finish line is ahead of you and it holds a blessing of eternal significance if you run the race with passion (Heb. 12:1).

Rico was faithful in every area he served and was honored accordingly.

When we die, will the angels rejoice? Will they salute and carry your soul into the presence of the Lord?

That will completely depend on what you do to make your life count *now*.

So the million-dollar question you need to answer is, are you going to *do something*?

ACTIVITIES

Close your eyes and imagine you're standing over your gravestone. Visualize your name on it. You are dead. Write down one aspect of your life that you now kick yourself for not being more faithful to God about. Make a decision today to do something about transforming that unfaithfulness into complete obedience. If you do, you will be well on your way to pleasing God and making your life count.

Dear Lord, I know that I soon will be standing in front of You to give an account for what I did with my life. I also realize that the only way I will hear "Well done, good and faithful servant" is if I have pleased You based on Your terms, not mine. I want to hear those words, God. Lord, I want to spend the rest of my life doing only that which makes life count in Your eyes. Thank You for giving me another chance to serve Your purposes in my life.

DO Something! Myth 6

I should expect tremendous suffering and difficulties. That's how I know I'm doing what God wants me to do.

The Lies Behind It

- God's work for us makes us miserable.
- The trials that come out of *doing something* leave us empty and burned out.

The Truth

- God will refine you through trials, but He will make it clear to you if you are fulfilling your purpose.

Scripture

Come to Me, all you who labor and are heavy laden, and I will give you rest. Take My yoke upon you and learn from Me, for I am gentle and lowly in heart, and you will find rest for your souls. For My yoke is easy and My burden is light.
—Matthew 11:28–30

Something to Remember

God specifically equipped you for mighty good works. It might be hard, but you should find it meaningful and inspiring. Being out of your comfort zone doesn't mean that you have to be out of your fun zone. I am on the most exciting journey of my life.

You

An Epilogue

Thirty-five hundred people packed out the 10:00 a.m. service. The crowd mirrored the socioeconomic and ethnic blend of San Diego. A friend once told me the Rock's mix of age, race, and class looked like how she envisioned heaven will be.

From the stage, I raised my hand and asked a series of simple questions.

"How many of you have ever abused drugs or alcohol?" Hundreds of hands went up.

"How many of you have ever done things sexually you wish you could undo?" (That's code for porn, adultery, lust, infidelity, molestation and rape, prostitution, whatever.) Hundreds of hands went up.

With each question, murmuring and gasps rolled through the audience as people began to realize how common their problems were—they were not alone. I got the sense that people felt more and more comfortable being open about their sinful drama. I went on.

"How many of you have ever been depressed?" (Code for overwhelmed with life.) Hundreds of hands went up.

"How many of you have ever wanted God to take you to heaven early?" (Code for contemplating suicide.) Hundreds of hands.

". . . worshiped your own form of God?" (Code for idolatry.) More hands.

". . . have been or know someone who has been arrested?" ". . . been guilty of hypocrisy?" ". . . have lied, cheated, been envious, acted out of jealousy or anger, stolen something, gossiped, or hated someone?"

Hands everywhere.

What about you?

If you can identify with any of the categories listed above, then raise your hand, right where you are. Right now. Go ahead. Don't worry, no one's looking.

You're Qualified!

Congratulations! If you raised your hand, you're qualified to do something to make your life count.

Jesus came to our world and clothed Himself with a human body, which ended up bloodied, beaten, and broken on the cross. He died, rose from the grave, and ascended to heaven—leaving behind broken people to do even greater things than He did (John 14:12).

We too are beaten, bleeding, and broken from life. Nevertheless, we are His chosen vehicle through which to fulfill His plan to bring love to a broken world.

You're Positioned!

You are not only qualified to do something, you are positioned.

Here's what I mean. You live in a world that needs God's love. As you travel through your world today, look at the brokenness that surrounds you. Anywhere you go, you're bound to see convalescent homes, jails, strip clubs, broken-down schools, foster group homes, women's shelters, homeless centers. Inside those places are drug addicts, fatherless children, gangbangers, abandoned seniors, the scared, the depressed, the ill.

You are standing there, facing a world that's in critical condition, that has had its limbs amputated, that is hurt and angry. Will you run the other way, like I did when I stood in front of Tracy, the twenty-five-year-old amputee in the hospital room? The difference is, now you are more qualified than I was. Instead of pride, you know to bring your brokenness to your patient. The brokenness that God needs and wants to love and transform into something powerful.

Are You Determined?

Since that awful day in the hospital, I have been on a mission to do something to make my life count. My prayer is that you would never experience the dreadful feeling of embarrassment I had running out of that hospital, leaving that girl in that bed suffering worse than when I walked in because I couldn't help her.

You represent that potential help to someone.

Remember what Jesus said: "Most assuredly, I say to you, he who believes in Me, the works that I do he will do also; and greater works than these he will do, because I go to My Father" (John 14:12).

That's not me talking, that's Jesus. I hope you have come to realize that you and Jesus have more in common than you thought. You may be convinced that He meant what He said. He is ready to do incredible things through you.

The question is, are you ready?

Look around you. *You* can see the need. You know someone needs to do something. *How* determined are you to be that someone?

Will you *do something* and make your life count?

Be Something

The first time I was cut from an NFL team was in 1982, two weeks before a players union strike. During the strike, the team practiced at a local park. I found that out the hard way. I was working out in the park with another former player when the team began to show up. After our workout, we spent a few minutes watching practice from the other side of the fence, talking about how much we deserved to be out there. We knew the plays, we were in shape, and it hurt to see, in our opinion, less talented guys living our dream. What made things worse, we weren't even allowed inside the fence. Being prevented from coming inside was not a talent issue. It wasn't about us being out of shape or not as skilled as the other players. It wasn't about whether we could do something. It was that we needed to be something. We needed to be on the official roster.

When it comes to heaven, there will unfortunately be people who end up on the outside looking in, and it won't be a talent or skill issue. People go to heaven, not because they attend church or because they are smarter or better than anyone else. It is not because they can do something special.

It is because they decided to be something:

Eternally forgiven.

We are all sinners, and the penalty of our sin is death, both physical and spiritual death. Because of our sin, we can never be good enough in our power to earn or deserve heaven.

Even though we cannot do something to earn heaven, we can decide to be something: eternally forgiven by the only One who died to pay the penalty for our sins—Jesus.

It is as simple as ABC:

A: Accept that you are a sinner and that your sin has a penalty of physical and eternal spiritual death (Rom. 3:23; 6:23).

B: Believe that Jesus is Lord; that because of His great love for you, He died to pay for your sins and rose from the dead to give you eternal life (Rom. 5:8).

C: Confess your sins and ask Jesus to forgive you (1 John 1:9; Rom. 10:9).

If you believe these ABC's of salvation, your next step is to say a prayer like the one below. But remember, you must have faith that God will honor your trust in His Word, forgive your sins, and send the Holy Spirit into your heart. Let me encourage you to be forgiven. Allow Jesus to do something spiritually eternal in you so He can do something spiritually eternal through you.

Dear Lord,
I acknowledge that I am a sinner.
I believe that Jesus is Lord, that He died to pay the price for my sins, and that He rose from the dead.
Jesus, please forgive my sins. I receive the Holy Spirit into my heart.
I pray this in Jesus' name.
Amen.

If you prayed that prayer, congratulations!

Now go to www.milesmcpherson.com for your next step!

Appendix A

The *DO Something!* Challenge

Within a ten-mile radius of the Rock Church in San Diego, besides 86 Starbucks, there are

- 12 abortion clinics
- 17 adult book and video stores
- 34 drug treatment centers (rehab)
- 7 homeless shelters
- 12 battered women's resource centers
- 425 AA meetings (every week!)
- 116 bars and nightclubs
- 280 liquor stores
- 58 escort services and strip clubs

In 2008, within ten miles of the Rock Church there were

- 23 murders
- 199 rapes
- 417 armed robberies
- 1,933 aggravated assaults
- 2,218 residential burglaries
- 4,845 motor vehicle thefts

Below is a map of "MyTown, USA." As you can see, our communities are in critical condition and in need of someone to do something. In 2009 the Rock Church set a goal to give 600,000 Do Something volunteers hours. Go to dosomethingworld.org for an update on what they did and how they did it.

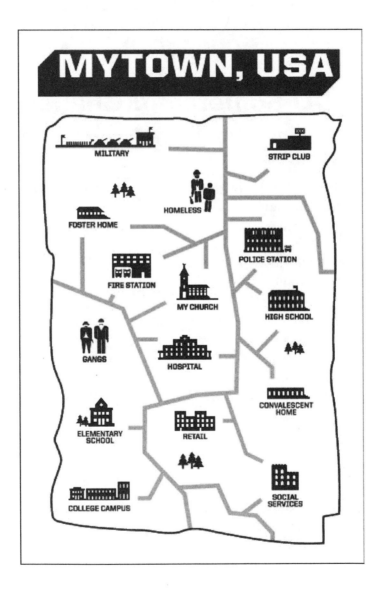

For a similar profile of your neighborhood, go to www.dosome thingchurch.org to see what's going on around *your* church, *your* home, *your* workplace.

Jesus Christ called His followers to take His good news of love and redemption into all the broken world. Are you doing that?

Acts 1:8 says, "But you shall receive power when the Holy Spirit has come upon you; and you shall be witnesses to Me in Jerusalem, and in all Judea and Samaria, and to the end of the earth."

The reason God has given you power is so you can do something in your community, wherever it is in the world. The best place to begin is at home, and taking the *DO Something!* Challenge is one way you can start.

I challenge you to do something! If twenty-five people from your church or community started twenty-five ministries, think how much of a difference that would make in your city—or town or village or neighborhood.

The needs of the people around you are endless, but here's a list of just twenty-five areas in which you and twenty-four other leaders can do something. All these and more can be found at www.dosomethingworld.org.

1. Ph.DO: Retail chaplains
2. Ph.DO: Homeless
3. Ph.DO: Strip clubs/adult industry
4. Ph.DO: Foster youth mentoring
5. Ph.DO: Deaf foster youth
6. Ph.DO: Cancer care ministry
7. Ph.DO: Domestic violence
8. Ph.DO: Human trafficking
9. Ph.DO: Prison
10. Ph.DO: Clothing/thrift emergency services
11. Ph.DO: Elementary school ministry
12. Ph.DO: Mentoring
13. Ph.DO: Makeup makeover
14. Ph.DO: Eating disorder
15. Ph.DO: Drug/alcohol recovery
16. Ph.DO: Military
17. Ph.DO: Convalescent homes

18. Ph.DO: The Work Ministry
19. Ph.DO: Home repair
20. Ph.DO: Recycling
21. Ph.DO: The Doll ministry
22. Ph.DO: Youth tutoring
23. Ph.DO: Disabilities ministry
24. Ph.DO: Dog lovers ministry
25. Ph.DO: Bikes for kids

Appendix B

AWCIPA

A Way to Pray

AWCIPA is a simple prayer format to help focus your prayer time. Here's what it stands for.

> **A** dmire and thank God.
> **W** ait quietly before God.
> **C** onfess your sin.
> **I** ntercede for others.
> **P** etition for yourself.
> **A** dmire and thank God.

The key is to spend a given amount of time in each category. Have a pen, paper, and a Bible with you. When God speaks, you need to write it down.

Another tip: Avoid jumping around from one topic to another.

For example, for Admire, you could read Psalm 8:9 and spend three minutes simply admiring and thanking God for all of the great things He has done in your life. Do not ask for anything, do not confess any sin—just thank Him.

Do something similar for each letter of AWCIPA. If you spend five minutes in each category, you will have spent a half hour in focused prayer. When is the last time you can say you have done that?

Here are more suggestions.

For "A," read Psalm 8:9 and spend three minutes simply admiring and thanking God.

For "W," read Psalm 46:10 and then sit quietly and listen to God speak to you. Write it down.

For "C," read 1 John 1:9 and then confess your sins to God.

For "I," read Philippians 1:3–6 and then pray for other people.

For "P," read Psalm 51:10–12 and then ask for a pure heart.

For "A," read Psalm 8:9 and then thank God for everything you can think of.

Note: Feel free to use your own verses for each prayer category.

Appendix C

The Plan and the Five P's

What to Remember about the Plan, Preparation,
Purpose, Pain, Power, and Passion

The Plan

*According to Jesus, You Were Created to Do Something Great
and God Has a Plan to Help You Do It.*

1. **Before you were born, God made all of the necessary preparations for you to do something that will make your life count.**

God has prepared you with every necessary natural and spiritual skill needed, along with the ideal opportunities in life to use those skills to help people. He is also prepared with all of the encouragement you will ever need to get you through the difficult times. You are more prepared than you know.

2. **God's purpose for your life is to love Him by simply doing something obediently.**

Your life will only count for something eternal if what you do is motivated by loving God. Loving God has nothing to do with emotion or feeling; it has everything to do with faith-based *obedience*. The only true measure of your love for God is your level of obedience to Him.

3. If you don't want pain merely to hurt, do something.

Pain can be described as the feeling associated with not getting what we want. The best thing we can do is want something different—something God wants.

If we decide, instead of avoiding pain, to pursue the lessons and personal growth pain is designed to bring to our lives, pain will do much more than just hurt. It will help you make your life count.

4. Power is the authority, ability, and opportunity to "do."

God has set aside all the power you will ever need. You cannot do something meaningful in the spiritual realm without spiritual power. But before you can acquire spiritual power, you must acknowledge and surrender your human power and strength. The more you surrender, the more you will be empowered.

5. Without the passion to do something, you will never complete your God-given mission.

Passion will see a light of hope in complete darkness. It is impossible to please God without faith, but there will be times in our life when even the God we put our faith in seems to have forsaken us. It is during those darkest of times that our passion stubbornly keeps believing that God is still there.

Preparation

The Extent God Has Gone to Prepare You to Live a Life That Counts

1. Before you were born, God prepared you by giving you a measure of faith.

Faith is a tool through which you could conduct a relationship with Him. Having created us as creatures who exercise faith every day, He prepared us in advance with the necessary ability to have a relationship with the unseen.

212

2. Before you were born, God prepared you with truth by giving you His Word, the Bible.

Just as in Jesus' case, before you needed to apply truth in your life, the basic guidelines for right and wrong on which to focus your obedience were already prepared. He prepared us with His Word, the Bible. Faith in God's Word is the quickest and surest way to do something of eternal significance in your life.

3. Before you were born, God prepared you by giving you the Holy Spirit to help you.

God prepared a Person, the Invisible Man, to be with us 24/7. He knew it would be impossible for us to be faithful if we were left alone, so He created us in His image so that we could have a relationship with Him through His Spirit. The Invisible Man will teach, encourage, guide, and convict you. He will pray for and love you like a best friend would—just better.

4. God has prepared us with prayer—communication with God that fosters a relationship with God.

Because God wanted a relationship with His children based on continuous interaction, He prepared us with the gift of prayer. Through prayer, we not only have two-way communication and the sharing of information but the sharing of the heart and character of God.

5. Before we were born, God prepared the circumstances of our lives to maximize our DO Something opportunities.

God has prepared "Do Something layups" for you with the people whose needs are tailor-made for the help He has prepared you to give. God is also prepared with all of the encouragement and motivation you will need in each and every "Do Something layup" situation. The more faithfully we take advantage of the do something opportunities presented to us, the more our life will count for something bigger than us.

Purpose

What Your Purpose Is, and What You Must Allow God to Do in Your Life to Equip You to Fulfill It

1. You cannot fulfill your purpose without a "heart transplant."

Fulfilling your eternal purpose begins with receiving a new heart, a spiritual heart transplant. God's ways are not our ways, and our natural tendency is to resist obeying Him. A spiritual heart transplant will provide a heart that desires to fulfill His purposes, not our own.

2. Fulfilling God's purpose for your life will require seeing people with eyes of love.

A new heart will reveal new truth about your world, the people in it, and most importantly, *you*. When you are able to see your own brokenness through God's love, you will be able to more clearly see and do something loving for the broken people in your life.

3. Fulfilling your purpose applies even toward the uninterested or those the world considers unlovable.

Your new heart will see the brokenness in your life and others. It will at the most unexpected time give its undivided attention to an unexpected person. God's love for the broken world never takes a break for anyone, especially those considered outcasts by the world.

4. Your purpose of expressing God's love will lead to receiving a lesson about God's love.

The biggest mistake we make in loving others is to forget about our own need to be loved and our need to learn *how* to love. If you can bring your brokenness along while loving others, especially to those considered "the least of these," you will receive a powerful lesson by Mr. Love Himself, Jesus.

5. Fulfilling your purpose will involve empowering others to fulfill theirs.

The ultimate affirmation that you have fulfilled your purpose is to have multiplied yourself in someone else. Just as human parents have biological children, so spiritual people make disciples—spiritual children.

Pain

The Benefits and Lessons God Has Intended Pain to Bring to Your Life.

1. Pain doesn't have to only hurt; it can also protect you from spiritual mistakes.

How often have you wished that you didn't have to hurt? Fortunately, God knows best. He gave us pain as a means of protecting us from not only harmful physical behavior but harmful spiritual behavior too. You need to ask yourself what spiritual lessons your pain is trying to teach you, and then do something in response.

2. Allow Jesus to speak directly to your pain—dealing with the cause, not the symptoms.

Often our reaction to our physical pain is guided by our flawed perspective on its cause and purpose. Getting the most out of our pain requires that we allow God to override our perspective and direct us to a spiritually accurate response.

3. No matter how much pain hurts, God will always provide an exit strategy.

We must be committed to who we are—the people God made us to be. Resist letting pain, or the people and circumstances causing pain, define you. If we remain committed to reacting to our pain as children of God and not as helpless victims, we will walk through it and do something significant in the world.

4. Pain doesn't have to only hurt, because it always provides ministry opportunities.

God prepares opportunities to do something and fulfill our purpose, even in painful situations. We need to keep our eyes open for who He will bring into our lives during our painful experiences. We cannot allow our brokenness to cause us to selfishly think only about ourselves.

5. **Enduring pain for others may hurt, but it will make you more like Jesus than anything else.**

When you suffer on behalf of others in Jesus' name, it will hurt, but know this: this pain, more than anything else, makes you like Jesus. Jesus told us to do only one thing in remembrance of Him: celebrate His pain. The one act that makes us most like Christ is our willingness to suffer on behalf of others.

Power

How to Acquire and Use the Spiritual Power God Has Set Aside for You

1. **Spiritual power comes when you surrender to God.**

When compared to the kingdom of man, the kingdom of God seems backward. This is no more evident than when it comes to the acquisition of power. Natural power is acquired by force, when one person takes it from another. In the kingdom of God, power is received when we surrender.

2. **The exercise of spiritual power validates your relationship with God.**

The biggest difference between someone who knows *about* God and someone who *knows* God is power. The first and most important display of God's power is its transforming influence over your brokenness.

3. **Spiritual power is to be used to transform our lives and those who need the same comfort we received.**

God's power transforms your life for two reasons: first, to reveal Himself to others through you; and second, to empower you to share that transformation with someone else. If you want to make your life count, find someone who hurts like you and bless them with the comfort that you have received.

4. **Your spiritual power will empower you to provide others with opportunities to minister.**

Sharing your powerful life-transforming experience to bless others is a noble task, but there's another step you can take. Just as God prepared opportunities for you to share His powerful transformation in your life, He can use you to prepare opportunities for others to share their powerful transformation.

5. **If you want big power, you need to make a big sacrifice.**

The more committed you are to doing something that matters to God, the more power you will need. And since in the kingdom of God power comes when you surrender, the more you surrender the more power you receive.

Passion

The Commitment Necessary to Complete What God Has Established for You to Do in Your Life

1. **Passion stakes its life only on the resources prepared by God.**

When everything in our lives seems to be falling apart, or when trusting God seems to have led us into difficult situations, it is our tendency to begin to make up our own rules—to trust our gut instead of God. Passion sticks to the plan and relies only on the guidelines established by God.

2. **Passion to fulfill our purpose blesses our enemies even while they are attacking us.**

Not even the hurtful, backstabbing behavior of our enemies can back down our passion to honor God with our lives and fulfill our purpose. Passion is so determined to help you fulfill your purpose that it will bless those who curse you even while they are in the very act of hurting you.

3. **Passion voluntarily walks into pain.**

A passion to never quit will walk into painful situations if obedience to God requires it. Passion is so determined to keep the eyes of our

217

faith on the lessons and power that result from our pain that it willingly walks into pain itself.

4. Passion converts God's power into self-control.

It is equally important for God's power to be applied in our own lives, as well as through our lives. Our passion to use God's power only according to God's plan ensures that we are subjected to it, as well as dispensers of it.

5. Passion eagerly anticipates the final approval of our Father in heaven.

Passion presses on to receive approval from God alone. Passion is what keeps us focused on crossing life's finish line in such a manner that He will say, "Well done, good and faithful servant." Only then can we say, "It is finished."

"Help Wanted" Notes

1. International Bulletin of Missionary Research (www.internationalbulletin.org)
2. Money.cnn.com/2009/01/09/news/economy/jobs_december/index.htm
3. www.ericdigests.org/1998-2/hard.htm
4. www.lsa.umich.edu/psych/news/department/news/?id=160
5. www.aacap.org/cs/root/facts_for_families/foster_care
6. www.pewcenteronthestates.org/uploadedFiles/One%20in%20100.pdf
7. www.usa.safekids.org/tier2_rl.cfm?folder_id=2020
8. www.nccp.org/profiles/US_profile_6.html
9. www.palace.net/~llama/psych/injury.html; http://selfinjury.org/indexnet.html; www.essortment.com/articles/self-injury_100006.htm
10. www.nichd.nih.gov/news/releases/bullying.cfm
11. www.usfa.dhs.gov/fireservice/fatalities
12. www.rainn.org/statistics
13. www.pamelaegan.com/articles/addiction.htm
14. www.cancer.org/docroot/cri/content/cri_2_6x_cancer_prevalence_how_many_people_have_cancer.asp
15. www.bayswan.org/stats.html
16. xxxchurch.com/gethelp/parents/stats.html
17. www.news-medical.net/?id=37529
18. www.ncsacw.samhsa.gov/files/508/3_Responding2Families.htm
19. www.bls.gov/oco/ocos158.htm#emply; www.bls.gov/oco/ocos160.htm#outlook; www.bls.gov/oco/ocos156.htm#outlook
20. U.S. Department of Justice (www.usdoj.gov)

Acknowledgments

I could not have put this book together without the contribution of many people. I want to first thank my wife for her patience through this writing process. It has consumed valuable time that frankly belonged to her.

Thank you, Deb. I love you very much.

I want to express gratitude to my staff for their prayers and support. They do something every day to make a difference in the world. Thanks also to Chad Allen, acquisitions editor at Baker Books, who caught the vision, and to my agent, Matt Yates.

Special thanks to Lynn Vincent and Sara Goetz for your insight and countless phone calls and conversations.

I also want to thank Pastors Matt Tague, Mark Hoffman, Kevin Mannoia, and Charlie Campbell. Also Dean Nelson, Ken Blanchard, Martha Lawrence, Renee Broadwell, Anna Espino, Barbara Hart, Anisha Jackson, Nora Barnes, Frank Vizcarra, Rob Pace, Tania Babaie, Richard Bagdazian, Jason Friesen, Dave Goodwin, Piper Nadelle, Brad Wilson, and Mori Bell.

Thank you to the generous people who shared their stories: Greg and Cindy Bradford; Donna and Bill Davis; Ken Davis; Tony and Jordan Dungy; Vincent and Vanessa Gabriele; Rio-Bec Hernandez; Michele Kassa; Beverly Kelly; Mindy Kurczodyna; Lisa Ortiz; Ricky, Nova, and Elisha Page; Noemi Preciado; David Rodgers; Mark Ruppert; Sherrill Naegele; Carl Ruthberg; Theresa Scher; Lisa Walker; Jessica Yaffa; Robert Yates; and the family of Federico "Rico" G. Borjas.

I want to thank Carrie Prejean, who I met after this manuscript was complete. You certainly Did Something courageous. Keep standing, "girlfriend."

I want to express a special thank you to my collaborator, Anita Palmer. Your wisdom and skill have brought this book to another level. I could not have done this without you. Thanks for being flexible and professional.